THE ART OF IMPACT

THE ART OF IMPACT

ACTION PRINCIPLES FOR A WORLD IN CRISIS FROM THE EXTRAORDINARY LIFE OF HANSJÖRG WYSS

PAUL ORZULAK AND SETH SCHULMAN

DISRUPTION BOOKS

New York Washington, DC

Published by Disruption Books
Washington, DC
www.disruptionbooks.com

Distributed by Disruption Books

For information about special discounts for bulk purchases, please contact Disruption Books at info@disruptionbooks.com.

Cover image © Shutterstock/Josemaria Toscano

Cover and book design by Sheila Parr

Library of Congress Cataloging-in-Publication Data available

Printed in the United States of America

Print ISBN: 978-1-63331-117-6
eBook ISBN: 978-1-63331-118-3

First Edition

CONTENTS

FOREWORD

VICE PRESIDENT AL GORE

"Something will have gone out of us as a people if we ever let the remaining wilderness be destroyed; if we permit the last virgin forests to be turned into comic books and plastic cigarette cases; if we drive the few remaining members of the wild species into zoos or to extinction. . . . We simply need that wild country available to us, even if we never do more than drive to its edge and look in. For it can be a means of reassuring ourselves of our sanity as creatures, a part of the geography of hope."

— An excerpt from Wallace Stegner's "Wilderness Letter," written to the Outdoor Recreation Resources Review Commission, December 3, 1960

A COMMON UNDERSTANDING AMONG the friends of Hansjörg Wyss is that when he reaches out, you never know from where in the world he might be calling.

He may have recently arrived at base camp on Mount Kilimanjaro or could be navigating the Amazon on a fact-finding trip in southeastern Peru. He may be visiting a midwife training center in Africa or running a board meeting at an art museum in Geneva. He could be leading a conversation on public lands in rural Montana, greeting Ukrainian immigrants at a center for refugee health in Philadelphia, exploring new immunotherapies for cancer with researchers in Boston, or touring a breathtaking natural monument on the North Rim of the Grand Canyon in Arizona.

I'm not sure what is more notable about each of these treks: that he maintains this level of activity well into his ninetieth year or that he always has such a profound impact on the places he visits.

Hansjörg embodies the fierce sense of purpose captured in the environmentalist and novelist Wallace Stegner's famous "Wilderness Letter" that I've quoted above. In fact, Hansjörg's clear-eyed approach to protecting our planet's precious biodiversity has led to the preservation of one hundred million acres of land! Incredibly, that is an area nearly equivalent to the entire nation of Sweden. And he recently pledged $1.5 billion to save the planet, making him one of the most significant conservationists of our time—indeed, of all time.

But here's the thing: Despite his achievements, you likely have never heard of Hansjörg Wyss. And one reason is that his goal is not to achieve acclaim; his goal is action.

I've had the pleasure of knowing Hansjörg for nearly thirty years. Our work together began in the early days of the Clinton–Gore administration, where he was a fierce and trusted ally in our efforts to protect some of America's most unique landscapes. His late partner, the brilliant Rosamund Stone Zander, was a lifelong friend and cherished collaborator whose passion and expertise were invaluable in her role on the board (which I chair) of the nonprofit Climate Reality Project.

So, I would like to tell you a little bit about this remarkable man you've probably never heard of, in this foreword to a terrific book about his life.

Hansjörg Wyss grew up in a working-class family in Switzerland, first traveling to the United States as a college student for a summer job in Colorado. I have listened, while pulling a canoe from the Caney Fork

River on my farm in Tennessee, as Hansjörg described his first summer in the majestic mountains of the American West with the reverence of a man whose life was forever changed by the experience.

That summer led him to build a life and career in America, where he started a medical device company that transformed orthopedic care. Throughout his accomplished career in business, Hansjörg never stopped living with the ethos of that young student exploring the West—traversing the country in his old, beat-up Subaru with that everlasting reverence for the natural beauty of our planet. Later, when he sold his company and became one of the wealthiest people in the world, he committed himself to the work of protecting the habitats and landscapes that have so deeply inspired his life and that he believes are essential to the future of humanity.

Hansjörg is a singular figure in the conservation world, and through the Wyss Foundation he has gathered some of the nation's brightest and most innovative minds to protect the planet's beautiful open spaces as public lands. He knows the hard work of conservation cannot be done by one person or one organization alone, and that knowledge remains a key to his success. His foundation has worked hand in hand with local and Indigenous communities, national governments, land trusts, and nonprofit partners to permanently protect those one hundred million acres of land along with more than three million square kilometers of ocean. No other person living on this planet today has been able to catalyze conservation action at this scale.

His expertise in building coalitions and sustaining grassroots support for conservation was invaluable to the efforts of the Clinton–Gore administration in creating nineteen new national monuments and expanding three others. With the help of Hansjörg, we were able to protect land covering about 5.9 million acres, the second most acres of any administration at the time. And when some of those national monuments came under threat, Hansjörg personally reconvened the network of groups that fought to preserve the land in the first place, seeking to prevent any reversal. Those groups' advocacy ultimately led to the passage of a new law that codified the National Landscape Conservation System so it would protect these historic lands forever.

Given the hard-fought successes of his philanthropy and advocacy in the United States, it should come as no surprise to learn that once Hansjörg fully retired from the business world, he massively scaled up his efforts to address the biodiversity crisis. Taking his work global, he pledged $1.5 billion to create the Wyss Campaign for Nature. Utilizing the expertise developed in his US-based campaigns, Hansjörg set out to rally support around the world for an agreement that would protect 30 percent of the planet's land and seas by 2030. In today's fractured geopolitical landscape, it is difficult to imagine bringing 190 countries together to agree to a common goal, but that's just what happened. In December 2022, the United Nations Biodiversity Conference passed what is considered the most significant commitment to biodiversity of its kind in history, in which all parties to the UN's biodiversity treaty agreed to work together to make the 30x30 pledge a reality.

Hansjörg's unwavering focus on conservation has yielded incredible successes, but it is not the only area where his impact has been felt. He has managed to find time to pioneer new approaches to medical research through the institutes he funds at Harvard University and three additional centers in Switzerland. He also supports dozens of initiatives to advance scientific research, economic opportunity, democracy, women's health, education, and art, among others.

In all his endeavors, Hansjörg's contributions go beyond the financial. He not only gives money but also devotes his time, his relentless attention, and his problem-solving ability to assuring the success of these charitable causes. He is living proof that as valuable as financial capital is, intellectual capital—the ability to ask questions, set goals, and transfer skills from one challenge to another—is just as essential in driving impact.

As you'll see in these pages, Hansjörg has a knack for coming up with creative ideas and novel strategies in real time. He has done so again and again throughout his life and career. In fact, that is why this book takes a unique approach to his life, going well beyond a traditional biography to answer some deeper questions: How does Hansjörg Wyss do what he does? And what principles and leadership lessons can we take away from his seventy-year career that might help us achieve similar results?

The story of Hansjörg's life, and the lessons that can be gleaned from his successes in meeting the challenges he has faced, has never been more relevant or urgent to understand. At a time when the twin climate and biodiversity crises are still growing worse faster than we are yet deploying their solutions, we risk falling victim to despair. In many ways, climate despair is the new climate denial. Fortunately, there is an antidote for this despair: action. And Hansjörg Wyss has shown time and time again what is possible when you choose to act. His story reminds us that anything is possible if we work hard, fight smart, stay focused, and do the work that needs to be done.

If Hansjörg Wyss has a secret weapon, it is this: He has never forgotten, as a person who grew up with very little in postwar Europe, what America has meant to the rest of the world, what it can still represent to the future of the planet, and what we must do together to create the better future we all hope to see. That's why he continues to do as much as anyone to save the waters, lands, and species of his adopted country and the world, for all his fellow citizens to appreciate. It's a sense of universal responsibility beyond constraints or categories, and beyond despair—a sense that what matters most isn't just that we have purple mountain majesties above the fruited plain but that our grandchildren and great-grandchildren one day have them too.

Hansjörg's work—on conservation, on groundbreaking medical research, on preserving the world's beauty as captured in its art, and on his other endeavors—is more than a noble use of his personal wealth. It's a profound expression of hope. It's a belief that no matter what threatens the world around us, we can still do something as individuals, as human beings, to bring about change even when others regard such efforts as futile. As Molly McUsic, Wyss Foundation president and longtime counselor to the secretary of the US Department of the Interior, once put it, Hansjörg Wyss reminds us of something crucial: "We don't have to be spectators in the causes we care about. We can fight. And once in a while, in spite of the human urge to bulldoze nature, in spite of all the money and power on the other side, we can win—and win on a scale that can make you cry."

That's what *The Art of Impact* is all about. I hope you find this journey across the "geography of hope" as unforgettable as the person who inspired it—wherever he may be calling from today.

INTRODUCTION

THE YEAR IS 1958. In the historic city of Bern, Switzerland, a college student notices a billboard announcing that the Colorado highway department is offering summer internships for engineering majors like him. The pay isn't great—about fifty dollars a week—and some of the student's friends tell him there's no way he'll be able to live in America on that. But this student is restless and pining for an adventure. He's eager, too, to see the United States, which (judging from movies and newspaper stories) seems to be glamorous, exotic, the center of the world.

This student understands how to live simply and economize. He grew up in very modest, lower-middle-class surroundings: His father was a calculator salesman, and the family made do in a tiny, third-floor walk-up with no refrigerator. Every day, this student lugged a smelly canister of oil up three flights of stairs from the basement so the family could have hot water. He decides to take a chance and apply.

Months later, he's on an economy-class Swissair flight to New York crowded with students. Arriving at John F. Kennedy International Airport, he makes his way to Long Island, where he'll stay with a host family before flying on to Denver. Little does he know that the days and weeks to come will be dizzying, eye-opening—every bit the adventure he is hoping for.

The night of his arrival, at a party at his host family's home, the student burns his poor European mouth on a hot pepper, the spiciest thing he has ever tasted. One of the guests, a plainclothes New York City police officer, watches him cough and gag and says, "Buddy, I feel for you."

At this officer's invitation, the student goes to a New York Yankees game, watching as some of the greatest players of all time take the field: Mickey Mantle, Whitey Ford, Yogi Berra. He knows nothing about baseball. He has barely heard of the game. But the officer takes it upon himself to teach the student the rules and strategies of America's pastime, and the student marvels to himself: Here he is, a new arrival, and already he knows the difference between a knuckleball and a fastball. Compared with the other Swiss students on the plane, he's *way* further along in his cultural immersion.

A couple of days later, he flies to Denver, where a woman greeting him at the airport helps him to arrange a place to stay for only $17.50 a week, including meals. The naysayers in Switzerland, with their provincial views, are proven wrong. In the United States, $50 goes surprisingly far. In fact, it will allow him not just to cover his living expenses but to buy a simple item he has always coveted: a folding garment bag to go with his suitcase.

When the student shows up for his internship at the highway department, he's assigned to work on a surveying crew comprised of men from the southern United States. Every weekday morning at six, the crew picks him up, and they drive into the Rocky Mountains to survey a new road being built near what is now the famous Coors brewery. At first, crew members treat him like a lackey, purposely accentuating their regional twang so he can't understand them. Soon, however, he gains their trust and shares some of what he learned the previous year in his surveying class. They grudgingly admit: This guy knows a thing or two.

On the weekends, the student does what he loves most: He laces up his hiking boots and heads out into nature. During his childhood, his parents liked to wedge him and his two sisters into the back of their tiny Fiat and take them on camping trips in the Swiss countryside. They set up tents by a lake, hiked, explored. In Bern, too, nature was always close at hand. The family's apartment was situated near a forest, and the student spent a great deal of time on his own there, playing during the summer and skiing in the winter.

Now, while working at the highway department, the student meets a librarian who makes a habit of taking the foreign interns in her Volkswagen bus on scenic trips around Colorado. They go to the Great Sand Dunes (then a national monument and now a national park), where they see swirling expanses of sunbaked sand ringed by distant mountains. They go hiking on Longs Peak in Rocky Mountain National Park, a mountain so rocky and austere that some have called it "a stone fortress in the clouds."[1] The kindness and generosity of this woman (and of Americans generally) astonish him. And she exposes him to scenery that moves him in ways that nothing ever has before.

Natural spaces in his native land, although undeniably beautiful, are manicured and bounded, planned with Swiss precision over many centuries. Evidence of human civilization is always present: a road, a telephone line, a farmer's field. In Colorado, for the first time in his life, the student encounters vast, wide-open spaces left in their natural state, with little if any evidence of human meddling. Best of all, this land is public and available for all to enjoy, something that isn't the case in Switzerland.

"I saw these huge vistas," he'll remember many years later. "I fell in love with the light. The sunsets were unbelievable, unlike anything I'd seen before. Every night, the colors were different. These huge landscapes, untouched. I fell in love with that country."

A LIFE'S WORK

We all experience epiphanies in our lives—episodes that transport and transform us. The Swiss engineering student, whose name is Hansjörg Wyss, didn't know it at the time, but he had begun a lifelong love affair with American culture, and particularly the American West. Far from the fifty dollars a week he lived on as an intern, he went on to become one of the world's wealthiest people, a self-made billionaire. He also became arguably the most effective and important conservationist in America since President Theodore Roosevelt started calling Americans' attention to the urgent need for a national system of protected lands a century earlier.

Through his philanthropic endeavors, Wyss has been responsible for preserving more than one hundred million acres across the United States as a public trust accessible to everyone. He has spearheaded a global campaign that successfully convinced 190 nations to commit to preserving 30 percent of Earth's land and oceans by 2030 (known as 30x30). Precious, irreplaceable natural wonders across the United States and around the world will be protected for future generations to enjoy—in the face of constant pressure by corporate real estate, mining, and energy interests—all because of him.

For nearly fifty years, Wyss served as chief executive officer (CEO) of a medical devices company that transformed an entire branch of medicine, turning recovery times for millions of patients from months to mere weeks. From that position, and with the wealth it brings, he dedicated himself to achieving significant, real-world impact at scale. In addition to protecting a landmass equal to the size of California and galvanizing a global conservation movement, he quietly revolutionized a dazzling array of other fields, including scientific research, public health, social justice, women's health, and the arts. Truth be told, he has likely touched the lives of more people in more places and in more ways than just about anybody else on Earth.

Despite the scale of that achievement, Hansjörg Wyss could be standing next to you and you wouldn't know it. Not only have you likely never *seen* Hansjörg Wyss; you probably had never *heard of him* until you picked up this book. Don't feel bad about that; his anonymity is not by accident but by design. In an era when everyone (particularly people in his position) seems to live their lives out loud, Wyss actively avoids the spotlight. He treasures his obscurity and privacy, delighting in his ability to walk down the street and make small talk with a grocery clerk, or grab a beer with a friend at a local café, without being recognized.

Wyss's travels have taken him as far as possible, in every way, from that three-story walk-up he lived in as a child, yet the truth is, he never really left it. He's still the student who knew how to make fifty dollars go far. He thinks of himself not as a billionaire but rather as an ordinary guy, on the same level as any of us and with the same claim to dignity and respect. A cynic might dismiss this as conceit. But Wyss's ordinariness is unmistakably genuine. While he enjoys some of life's finer things, he lives simply in most regards.

THE MOST IMPACTFUL PERSON YOU'VE NEVER HEARD OF

This book tells the story of the most impactful person you've never heard of—someone whose pronounced *ordinariness* is precisely what has made him so *extraordinary*. Throughout childhood, as the book repeatedly describes, Wyss pushed himself hard to learn and grow, as many middle-class kids do. But he took it much further, demonstrating an unending need to challenge himself, accomplish greater goals, and even drive social progress.

During the mid-1960s, Wyss returned to the United States and earned an MBA from Harvard Business School. More than a decade later, after working in management jobs around Europe, he returned once again and built a life for himself while running a small, struggling medical devices company with its headquarters in Pennsylvania.[2] That company, Synthes, grew precipitously, transforming the practice of orthopedics in the process. The company's technology revolutionized the way broken bones were treated, saving thousands of hours of recovery time and millions of dollars for patients, and making Hansjörg Wyss increasingly wealthy. At every opportunity, Wyss continued to enjoy the American West, going on extended treks with friends in Utah, Arizona, and elsewhere. With the help of many from the conservation community, he also started to do his part to protect the wild Colorado landscapes he fell in love with years earlier.

During the 1980s and early 1990s, Wyss made small-scale donations to environmental groups in the West dedicated to preserving open space for public use. During the mid-1990s, he began to fund citizens' groups working to protect local landscapes from development. By the late 1990s, he had taken his conservation efforts to a whole new level, creating a charitable foundation called the Wyss Foundation, which focused on protecting public lands. Wyss funded the foundation with millions of dollars, bringing in bright, energetic policy experts to staff it.

During the 2000s, when policymakers in Washington, DC, seemed bent on reversing environmental gains made under a previous presidential administration, Wyss ramped up funding for grassroots efforts across the United States, helping to launch a network of local groups passionate about protecting public lands and advocating for smart, sensible conservationist policies. Partnering with governments and leading environmental organizations, he helped to increase the amount of government-owned land that received protection—sometimes purchasing it outright and transferring it to government agencies, and sometimes using other legal means to ensure that the land wasn't developed or exploited. Most notably, Wyss worked with governments and local communities to protect hundreds of thousands of acres in the Crown of the Continent, a vast natural system stretching from Montana into Canada.

All along, Wyss would continue to increase his wealth. By 2011, Synthes became a wildly successful enterprise with billions of dollars in sales.[3] The following year, having retired as the company's CEO, Wyss sold it to an even larger corporation—Johnson & Johnson—for almost $20 billion, becoming one of the world's wealthiest people. Rather than blow this windfall on megayachts and mansions, he publicly pledged to give away most of his wealth.

Privately, he planned to do even more. He would take the time to learn about pressing needs, carefully select which projects to fund, and see to their good governance. He would visit conservation projects, traveling to Argentina, Chile, Kenya, Zimbabwe, and Romania as well as to lands in the United States. In short, Wyss would pursue his philanthropy with the same vigor, focus, and discipline he applied in running his business.

During the 2010s and 2020s, Wyss spent hundreds of millions, and then billions, conserving pristine wilderness around the world, mobilizing tactics like those that had worked in the United States. Rather than keeping this land private and locking it away behind fences and gates, he partnered with local communities and governments to preserve it as a public trust accessible to the people. He became an outspoken advocate, warning of the threats facing our remaining natural spaces, and challenging the world to preserve 30 percent of all land and sea globally within a decade's time. To raise awareness and generate public excitement, he pledged $1.5 billion to launch a global campaign to fund the protection of wild spaces. Through a partnership with environmental experts, delegates at the United Nations (UN) Biodiversity Conference in 2022 were persuaded to adopt the 30x30 challenge as their goal. All of this would amount to, in the words of one environmentalist, "a scale of conservation that we haven't seen ever attempted before."[4]

Always a realist, Wyss acknowledged that none of these accomplishments, however important, were remotely enough. As environmental perils continued to worsen, he doubted whether humanity would survive the ongoing degradation of our only home. But he continued safeguarding land for future generations. He took pleasure in knowing that at least he tried to make an important difference with the means at his disposal. Through the Wyss Foundation, he spent hundreds of millions every year funding hundreds of projects in dozens of countries. Given the scope of these projects and considering his decades-long business career, it's clear that hundreds of millions of people's lives are better because of his commitment to bringing about positive change.

Synthes wasn't his only avenue for improving health care and medical innovation. Over the past two decades, Wyss has spent about $750 million to found and support the Wyss Institute for Biologically Inspired Engineering, a first-of-its-kind academic center at Harvard University dedicated to taking great ideas that might otherwise have stayed in the ivory tower and turning them into a new generation of practical innovations. Wyss also has contributed hundreds of millions more in funding to create two similar academic centers in Switzerland. To date, these three centers have produced dozens of powerful innovations, including a wearable mask that diagnoses Covid-19; new treatments for conditions like cancer, pancreatitis, and infectious diseases; a brain-computer interface that lets paralyzed people communicate; technology that reverses the aging process in cells; and a novel way to seal internal wounds. Perhaps even more significant, these centers have pioneered a whole new model for conducting scientific research, one that breaks down disciplinary boundaries and focuses on what matters most: getting lifesaving treatments more quickly into the hands of patients who need them.

And that's not all.

Through an organization called the AO Alliance, Wyss has spread lifesaving orthopedic care to more than thirty developing countries in Africa and Southeast Asia. In the United States, his foundation supports numerous local and national groups that help underserved populations, including advocacy groups that fight predatory lending and unfair economic policies, a think tank aimed at addressing systemic inequality, a center that researches how to better support low-income families, a shelter in Maine that rescues victims of domestic violence, a group in Boston that provides emergency meals to women in crisis, an organization in Pennsylvania that delivers affordable mental health care and essential health services specifically to refugees and immigrants, and a group that serves at-risk kids in Wyoming, to name but a few.

An avid art collector, Wyss also has worked to make art more accessible to people worldwide. He provides major support to the Fondation

Beyeler, one of Switzerland's most popular art institutions, and routinely loans pieces from his personal collection to museums around the world so that anyone can enjoy them. In fact, Wyss has done more than just about anyone to further progress in public health, social justice, and the arts, both in the United States and around the world.

A POPULIST PHILANTHROPIST

You might wonder how a guy from a humble background—a man who'll tell you he never dreamed he could have had such influence—could come to achieve so much, distinguishing himself among the ranks of the world's most important philanthropists and business leaders. Wyss's success doesn't just reflect his wealth; others in his position haven't accomplished nearly as much. Nor, as Wyss is quick to note, does it reflect unusual intellect: He was an average student at school. And it doesn't stem from specialized knowledge in his areas of philanthropic interest. Initially inexperienced as a conservationist, and with little formal training in scientific research, medicine, or the arts, he just learned as he went.

Wyss would happily chalk his accomplishments up to luck. If you press him, though, he'll acknowledge that he does have certain talents relevant to business and philanthropy, such as an ability to organize people and a knack for analyzing businesses and spotting opportunity. The more acquainted you become with Wyss, the more you realize there's a deeper, more intriguing explanation—one with wide application for anyone seeking to make positive change.

As this book argues, Wyss managed to have unprecedented impact across domains because of an old-fashioned, middle-class sensibility rooted in a respect for the pragmatic and the everyday. Although he has traveled the world many times over, he still harbors many of the traditional values he learned as a child growing up in Bern. In Wyss's world, you don't waste the resources at your disposal. You look out for the vulnerable and underprivileged. You strive to achieve, challenging yourself intellectually and expanding the horizons of others around you. You avoid every species of bullshit, pretension, and elitism. Above all, you feel an abiding sense of gratitude for what you have, regarding your accomplishments not just as the fruit of individual effort but, in some deeper sense, as gifts conferred by society. You take on a sacred obligation to give back what Thomas Jefferson once called "a debt of service due from every man to his country, proportioned to the bounties which nature and fortune have measured to him."[5]

As mentioned earlier, Wyss's ordinariness is what has made him so clearly extraordinary—a paradox that holds true especially in relation to a particular facet of his middle-class sensibility: his aspirational mindset and desire for accomplishment, whether it's hiking new landscapes, meeting new people, taking on new projects, or discovering new art. But that sensibility has also informed his efforts in less obvious ways. Casting a skeptical eye on abstract theories and faddish "wisdom," he has crafted a unique approach both to running a business and to doing good. His attitude is pragmatic, commonsensical, performance-oriented, and aspirational. Whereas many of his fellow philanthropists give with an eye toward staying in the limelight, Wyss retains an old-school focus on what really matters: *results.*

To that end, Wyss involves himself in the details, just as he did when running Synthes. He cuts through bureaucracy, ensures that nothing is wasted, and makes practical adaptations to get the job done. He spots and aggressively pursues opportunities for positive change that others haven't yet grasped, always driving to transcend and improve. Spend any time visiting the lands he has helped to conserve or the communities he has empowered, and you realize the incredible results of his middle-class pragmatism and respect for everyday people: an impact on nature and humanity that is soaring, liberating, even poetic.

NOT YOUR USUAL BIOGRAPHY

As friends and former employees acknowledge, Hansjörg Wyss may be virtuous, but he's not perfect. He can be demanding, insensitive, and maddeningly unpredictable. He has blind spots like the rest of us. He suffers no fools and is legendary for his toughness. But these fellow travelers also affirm how fundamentally kind the man is and how much they've learned from him. Their stories and insights made it abundantly clear that alerting a broader public to his contributions while sharing his distinctive practices and values would be a worthy endeavor.

The Art of Impact is an authorized biography based on extensive interviews with Wyss and others around him. But it's not your usual biography. What's so remarkable about Wyss's life is that he achieves extraordinary results in wildly different disciplines by adhering to a set of core principles and commonsense insights that guide him. For this reason, instead of offering a conventional narrative of the man's life and legacy, this book highlights a selection of these action principles, grouping them so they illustrate three key areas of Wyss's impact—revolutionary business innovation, dedication to saving nature, and commitment to social justice—while also allowing for a roughly chronological narrative. Organizing the material in this way is intended not merely to bring attention to one of today's most inspiring yet mostly unknown philanthropists but also to inspire and enable further progress.

It's easy to blame others when change-making efforts fail to bear fruit: *Our opponents are too strong. Countervailing beliefs or interests are too entrenched. Our community is too distracted.* Although such statements might be true, it's also vital to look inward, noticing our own practices or ways of thinking that might be hampering our efforts. Here, Wyss's story can help. Just as he helped to pioneer internal fixation as a way of healing bone fractures, so the core principles behind his success can offer a "fix" for activists everywhere—a solution that maximizes their impact by strengthening their work *from the inside.*

Above all, Wyss's example reminds us that forward momentum

remains possible so long as we remain cognizant of our social responsibilities and resist a paralyzing pessimism. Any of us can use the principles informing his work to pursue a noble mission, whether we have one dollar or a billion dollars at our disposal. By tuning out the noise and committing to a serious, commonsense focus on mission and results, we can do more to heal society and our natural world. And as any number of stories from Wyss's life suggest, we can also reap the personal satisfaction, expansiveness, and joy that a life of service can bring.

Today's culture glorifies consumerism over charity, selfishness over service, vanity over virtue. But life is more than an endless drive for dollars and social media likes. We all have an opportunity to give back, whether by conserving nature, raising up the underserved, furthering science and innovation, or contributing to many other worthy endeavors. Let's rededicate ourselves to doing our best and performing service to society that is commensurate with what nature and fortune have given us. Ultimately, Wyss's greatest message takes the form of a simple question directed at common—and uncommon—people everywhere: What impact will *you* have?

PART I

REVOLUTIONIZING ORTHOPEDICS

1

THE VIRTUES OF BEING "CRAZY"

Cultivate a critical mindset that allows you to spot hidden opportunities—and disregard anyone who questions your sanity.

FOR MUCH OF THE twentieth century, an injury as common as breaking your leg on a ski slope or fracturing your ankle on a basketball court would have taken a terrible toll on your health and well-being. Standard practice for broken limbs in Western countries was to put you in a plaster cast or in traction, completely immobilizing your joint until the bone could regrow and heal. Although fractures weren't usually life-threatening, recovering from them usually meant putting your life entirely on hold and spending weeks (or more likely months) flat on your back in a hospital bed. Meanwhile, you accumulated serious medical bills and subjected yourself to hospital-borne infections—just because you happened to get too far over your skis or take an awkward step while going in for a layup. Spending weeks in a cast or in traction also caused your muscles to atrophy and your affected joints to become stiff, so you'd also have to commit to many more weeks of rehabilitation once the cast was removed and you could start moving about.

Today, orthopedic surgeons treat fractures very differently. Rather than immobilizing the affected extremity, they surgically implant highly engineered, precision metallic devices that fasten broken bones together, helping them to heal. With these "internal fixation devices," as they're called, most patients are back on their feet within a few days—no suffering through a lengthy hospital stay nor the cost, inconvenience, and health risk that accompany it. The adoption of these medical devices and new surgical principles and methods transformed orthopedic surgery during the 1980s and 1990s, and it wouldn't have been possible without the pioneering work that Hansjörg Wyss did as CEO of Synthes.

Although we take internal fixation for granted today, Wyss's decision to help commercialize the innovation represented quite a risk on his part. If you were a seasoned business manager with a Harvard MBA during the late 1970s and early 1980s and you were pondering your next career move, you probably wouldn't be looking to join a small company nobody has heard of in an industry that's unfamiliar to you. You certainly wouldn't want to join a medical device start-up on the brink of bankruptcy—one that had little patent protection, faced strong competition, and had no control over the manufacturing and cost of its products—all in exchange for a low salary. Yet that's precisely what Hansjörg Wyss did upon joining Synthes USA, the American subsidiary of Swiss medical device company Synthes, in 1977.[6]

Upon graduating from Harvard Business School in 1965, Wyss worked in a series of management positions in the United States and Europe. After a stint at Burlington Industries' management training program in New York, he became director general of a Swedish textile firm owned by Burlington, leading a successful turnaround of its business. Then, while still only in his early thirties, he took a big job overseeing sales, marketing, product development, and technical service for Monsanto's European fiber division, a $150 million business at the time. He stayed at Monsanto for seven years, amassing a strong record of success.

In 1975, unhappy with the career opportunities available to him, he left Monsanto and applied for senior leadership jobs at other firms. Within months, he was a finalist for the position of CEO at the Swiss food company Danone, and he also landed an attractive offer to work as president of a Swiss steel company. As Wyss tells it, his prospects at Danone faltered after he underwent evaluation by a French psychologist as part of the interview process. The psychologist asked him what legacy he'd like to leave after his death, to which Wyss replied, "I really don't care what people think of me after I'm gone." His reasoning, to which he subscribes even in old age, was that despite what people might hope, others don't remember us for very long once we have died. Concern with legacy is therefore a needless distraction. Hearing such an unsentimental view, the psychologist advised Danone's board of directors against hiring him, arguing that Wyss's disregard for his own legacy meant that he wouldn't work as hard on the company's behalf.

In the meantime, Wyss's hobby of flying airplanes had led him to become acquainted with the four surgeons who founded Synthes. As a side gig, he had begun buying planes in the United States and reselling them to European customers. One of those customers was Synthes cofounder Dr. Walter Kaufmann. Recognizing Wyss's business acumen, Kaufmann asked him to attend some Synthes business meetings and soon brought him on as a part-time consultant. In 1977, impressed by Wyss's strategic thinking, Kaufmann and his partners asked Wyss to run Synthes USA in exchange for a small salary and an equity stake.

For a young, up-and-coming manager like Wyss, the organizational complexity that surrounded Synthes USA might have been enough to raise serious alarm bells. Although the company was a for-profit enterprise, it grew out of the Swiss study group Arbeitsgemeinschaft für Osteosynthesefragen (Association of the Study of Internal Fixation), commonly referred to as AO/ASIF.[7] Founded in 1958 by Swiss surgeons and scientists, AO/ASIF was dedicated to the improvement of care for fractures and the restoration of patients to their pre-injury state as quickly as possible. Believing the surgical treatment of fractures led to much better results than the immobilization techniques that were widely used at the time, these surgeons conducted research at a lab in Davos, Switzerland, experimenting with new internal fixation tools and techniques that fixed and fastened the affected bones. By 1960, they were offering professional courses in the revolutionary treatment of fractures using these techniques. They also established a technical group that oversaw and approved new devices for use in surgically treating fractures and that put out publications spreading knowledge about internal fixation procedures.[8]

In 1960, members of AO/ASIF established a for-profit entity called Synthes Chur to market the innovative implants and tools created by AO/ASIF doctors.[9] The point was not to make Synthes Chur the next billion-dollar company but rather to position it as a tool to help effect a revolution in orthopedic surgery while also generating revenue to fund the doctors' ongoing research and educational pursuits. Consequently, Synthes Chur channeled all of its earnings back to AO/ASIF. In this way, AO/ASIF remained as free as possible of commercial influences, allowing the doctors to focus on furthering the science of internal fixation.

During the 1960s, Synthes Chur enlisted two Swiss companies, Mathys and Straumann, to manufacture its products, and these companies in turn negotiated for the rights to market the products they manufactured in exchange for royalty payments to Synthes. The arrangement worked well in Europe, with Synthes making headway in countries like Germany and Austria. In one German hospital, the number of internal fixation procedures rose by a factor of seven during the 1960s.[10] In the US market, however (which Straumann oversaw), sales growth was disappointing. Doctors remained suspicious of the idea of treating fractures surgically; they preferred the traditional method of immobilizing broken joints.

To remedy the situation, AO/ASIF established Synthes USA in 1974 as a separate entity to sell its products in the American market. But by

1977, when the doctors offered Hansjörg Wyss the chance to run the company, sales in the United States still weren't taking off, hovering at only around $5 million.[11] The problems were many: Synthes USA had a lackluster staff and inadequate leadership. When first interviewed by Hansjörg Wyss, the general manager said that he felt out of his depth. The fees that Synthes USA paid to Straumann for manufacturing its products seemed excessive, and renegotiating them wouldn't be easy. Financially, Synthes USA was struggling under a mountain of debt. All these factors made Synthes USA seem like a rather hopeless case—certainly not a job opportunity of the caliber available to Wyss elsewhere.

Upon hearing that Wyss had signed on at Synthes USA, Egon Zehnder, the legendary Swiss headhunter and management consultant who had placed Wyss in the steel company job, didn't mince words: He told Wyss he was "crazy." Zehnder called Wyss, insisting that he was making a massive mistake, and said he would never again take on Wyss as a client. Wyss countered by challenging Zehnder to have breakfast with him ten years later to the day, when he would inform Zehnder of how things at Synthes were working out. Wyss was confident he'd have a positive story to tell.[12]

When Wyss agreed to join Synthes USA, he believed in his decision so deeply that he also decided to put a sizable chunk of his life savings into acquiring a 20 percent ownership stake. He saw that for all the troubles facing the start-up, it represented "an unbelievable opportunity." There was little question about how successful Synthes's internal fixation devices already were in Europe. The problem in the United States was that "American orthopedic surgeons were ten years behind the rest of the Western world." Wyss thought it was inevitable that doctors in the United States would adopt internal fixation as a solution, if only because patients and the lawyers representing them would demand it. His challenge would be to put Synthes USA in the best possible position to take advantage of this massive transition waiting to happen. If he could do that, he felt convinced that great things would happen. He even thought he could build

Synthes USA into a global company, growing first in the United States and then eventually acquiring or merging with Mathys and Straumann.

Beneath this uncommon level of conviction lies one of the keys to Wyss's extraordinary impact: his remarkable ability to spot opportunities that others don't see.

THE PILOT WHO RAN A FACTORY

When Wyss was eighteen years old, he got a job shoveling sand and hauling bricks on a construction site run by one of Switzerland's largest builders. Almost immediately, he noticed how inefficiently the site was run. Because nobody had thought to order concrete at the appropriate times, workers found themselves standing around for hours on end with nothing to do. The site could be far more efficient if the company ordered supplies in a more thoughtful, organized way. Wyss brought this opportunity for improvement to his manager, who right then and there took Wyss off the front line and assigned him to an office job helping to run the site.

Wyss's skill at identifying opportunities was matched by his ability to size up looming threats, a talent he demonstrated early when he took interest in his father's job selling calculators. Most calculators like the ones his dad sold in the 1950s were mechanical—they relied on the physical movement of mechanical parts (often via a hand crank) to make calculations. During Hansjörg Wyss's first trip to the United States in 1958, however, he encountered a new, electronic calculator manufactured in Japan that greatly outperformed its mechanical counterparts. Wyss realized immediately that this technology would disrupt the market for mechanical calculators. Upon returning to Switzerland, he took the liberty of telling the owner of his father's company that unless he switched over to selling electronic calculators, he'd go out of business in a few years. The owner wasn't impressed. As Wyss recounts, "He told my father, 'Your son knows nothing, and I don't like him talking to me like that.'" Sure enough, a few years later—just as his father was slated to retire—the company went out of business.

But as Synthes CEO, Wyss had wide latitude to act based on his intuitions, which in turn allowed him to make any number of forward-looking decisions that might have struck others as strange or risky. For example, if you led a manufacturing company, would you ask a professional pilot you happened to meet at an airport to be a product manager? Would you then hire him to run a major manufacturing plant in another country? You would if you were Hansjörg Wyss.

In October 1982, Wyss happened to be at a tiny airport in Coatesville, Pennsylvania, when he saw a small notice advertising flight instruction offered by a man named Paul McMinn. Wyss met McMinn and was surprised to learn that when he wasn't flying, he practiced as a trained dental technician who ran a small laboratory with two employees. At the time, Synthes was starting a maxillofacial division that was making surgical implants to treat fractures of the skull and facial bones. Wyss discovered that McMinn could fabricate crowns and other dental implants, which gave Wyss an idea: Perhaps McMinn could use his dental fabrication skills to help design Synthes products.

Wyss hired McMinn as both a pilot and a product manager. Within a few years, having realized that McMinn was highly intelligent, deeply understood Synthes products, and was a gifted communicator, Wyss made him a regional sales manager—even though McMinn had never worked in sales. He also gave McMinn his personal plane to use when traveling to meet customers. McMinn excelled in this role, and some years later, when Wyss needed someone to run a new factory in Tuttlingen, Germany, he put McMinn in charge—again, despite McMinn's total lack of relevant experience. McMinn wound up running the factory for years, producing excellent results.

Reflecting on this early judgment call and his relationship with McMinn, Wyss explains that he acted on intuition, sensing this pilot's potential based on their initial conversations. Wyss wasn't afraid of failure, because a flop (in his view) would have no serious repercussions. If McMinn didn't work out, Wyss could always reassign him to a different job—Wyss's standard practice when an employee showed potential but was underperforming—or, as a last resort, could usher him out of the company. Throughout his time at Synthes, Wyss consistently applied this intuitive, opportunity-oriented approach to hiring, sensing that individuals might have potential and then giving them a chance, regardless of what was printed on their résumés. Most of the time, Wyss's instinct proved correct and the individuals thrived, lifting the company with them.

CREATIVE SYMBIOSIS

An even more powerful way Wyss applied his opportunity-spotting abilities at Synthes was by overseeing research and development (R&D). CEOs at large companies tend to spend their time on tasks such as relationship building, strategic planning, and culture building while overseeing specific business units and functions across the organization.[13] Wyss oversaw these areas, but he prioritized R&D, allocating about one-third of his schedule to it. Wyss didn't design new products himself, sitting before a whiteboard and waiting for ingenious ideas to hit him. Instead, he understood his role to be that of a *curator* of ideas. He personally reviewed prototypes and designs for new internal fixation tools and devices that members of his R&D team created, deciding which ones to fund and which to shelve. He had a knack for spotting in an instant whether an idea held promise—not necessarily as a business proposition but as a means of serving surgeons better and advancing patient care. If an idea seemed sound, he didn't hesitate to write a big check, confident that the business consequences would ultimately be positive.

One of Wyss's closest collaborators in product development was Robi Frigg, whom Wyss first met in 1983. A trained mechanic who had never received a college degree, Frigg was working at the time as a photographer for the R&D arm of the AO/ASIF. He had an energetic, creative mind, particularly when it came to engineering or technical matters. Wyss became aware of this talent and, in 1988, brought Frigg to work at Synthes for a two-year stint, charging him with building out the company's R&D function, which Wyss had initially created within a year or two of his own arrival. Previously, the AO/ASIF had conducted R&D exclusively in Switzerland, and during Wyss's tenure it continued to do so in parallel to development activities at Synthes USA. Frigg would continue to work at Synthes during the 1990s and 2000s, acquiring over two hundred patents and becoming the company's chief technology officer.

As Frigg notes, a synergy took hold between him and his boss. Wyss gave him free rein to think up fresh ideas for new products or technical innovations for existing ones, and then picked out concepts that seemed especially promising for further development. Again, rather than selecting products based on pure revenue potential, Wyss looked for those that would solve clinical problems, understanding that sales would eventually follow.

To Frigg, Wyss's support for his creativity and risk-taking was quite special. "It's always extremely expensive to develop a technical product in the medical sector, and you run a great risk because you never really know if it works in the end," Frigg recalled years later. "If I had to ask a committee whether I was allowed to go on working on a specific tool, I'd never have gotten their permission, because there's no [guarantee] that it [will be] a success. But Hansjörg was always prepared to run that risk because he saw which of the implants was a potential success. He also never asked how much something was going to cost."

When Wyss saw potential in unorthodox, seemingly crazy ideas, he didn't hesitate to push hard for them, even in the face of internal resistance. One of the best examples, Frigg notes, was an innovative surgical plate Frigg developed in 1998 with holes that could accommodate two very different kinds of screws surgeons might use when repairing fractures. Traditionally, surgeons used compression screws, so called because to ensure that the plate was closely fixed to the bone, the doctors had to tighten the screws, compressing the plate tightly against the bone. The surface of the bones wasn't always perfectly flat, so this action sometimes prevented the fractured areas of bone from being held closely together, or it caused portions of bone to buckle outward. Locking screws were designed to solve this problem by literally locking into place on the plate itself, potentially even in the absence of tight contact between the plate and the bone. Research showed that locking screws were more effective clinically, allowing for a range of advantages. Still, surgeons resisted them out of habit, thanks to decades of training and experience with compression screws.

Frigg's drilled plate was uniquely designed to nudge surgeons toward adopting the new locking screws, as the plate could be used with both those and the traditional screws. Surgeons could use traditional screws most of the time, but in situations where a patient's bone was weak, they could decide in the moment to try locking screws without having to use a different, unfamiliar plate. To AO/ASIF surgeons, this innovation seemed uninteresting at first: Frigg could find only one sales representative in Europe and Asia who was willing to work with a surgeon to conduct clinical trials of the new plate. But Wyss was interested. Perceiving locking screws as the wave of the future, he asked Frigg to formally present his idea to a large group of senior leaders at Synthes USA.

"There was absolutely no interest among these leaders," Frigg later recalled. "It was as if they were sleeping. But Hansjörg stood up and said, 'We're doing this. We will take as our goal converting all clinics in the United States to this new plate.' It was a huge shift. And not long thereafter, Synthes did successfully convert clinics worldwide to the plate with this new [type of] hole in it. It was a [completely] new world in orthopedic surgery with this plate."[14]

Take an innovation like this and multiply it across years and decades, and you begin to understand why, by the 2000s, Synthes not only had expanded its sales exponentially and become a global company but was also widely regarded as the biggest innovator in its space.

ASKING TOUGH QUESTIONS

What's the secret to spotting opportunities the way Wyss does? How can the rest of us learn to adopt this approach to make our own advocacy even more impactful? The short answer: Question conventional wisdom, trust your instincts, allow yourself to think differently, and follow the path less traveled—or not yet traveled at all. Wyss wasn't afraid to be a first mover if he saw an opportunity that nobody else did. He made smart, farsighted decisions that sometimes would strike others as unorthodox, because he was looking at the world from a different perspective than most of us do.

Marcey Olajos, Wyss's longtime friend and former romantic partner, notes that Wyss always takes a big-picture view of every project or problem he's working through. In the context of environmental conservation, for instance, she explains, "He always goes beyond a particular problem or something that we're facing, like drilling for oil or something, and expands on it. It's because of this that the [Wyss] foundation has grown and gone global after starting very small. Whether it's business or philanthropy, it's always a big-picture view. That's how he looks at things."[15]

Even more fundamentally, Wyss cultivates what might be described as "ingrained nonconformism"—a constant inclination to disregard convention and question everything. Throughout his life, Wyss has challenged the status quo—in business, philanthropy, and even his personal life. Because he's always asking questions, thinking critically, and taking nothing for granted, he sees past the blind spots that so often impair others. He recognizes and in turn seizes on opportunities to make a difference that others can't yet fathom.

Wyss's friend and Harvard Business School classmate Mead Wyman regards Wyss's critical bent as pivotal. "I think that the secret of his success lies in the fact that he is an independent thinker," Wyman says. "Anything he undertakes, he tries to do in the best possible way. He is not restricted by standard values of society." Interestingly, it is Wyss's tendency to think critically that got him his job at Synthes in the first place.

Wyss remembers how, at one point while Dr. Kaufmann and the

other Synthes cofounders were courting him for the job, a Synthes USA representative came to Switzerland to give a presentation about the company and its performance. "It was very impressive, very fancy, with lots of slides and charts," Wyss recalls. "Afterward, I was asked to comment, and I told the four doctors and their financial advisor that the US operation was probably dead."[16] Wyss proceeded to alert the others to the problems he saw, including the lack of patent protection and the rise of competitors. Because he didn't simply accept what Synthes USA leaders said at face value and instead offered alternative views that were fresh and well reasoned, the Synthes cofounders gave him what turned out to be the opportunity of a lifetime.

Throughout his tenure at Synthes, Wyss's critical mindset influenced his leadership and the way he received ideas from others. He was known to be tough. If you were presenting your ideas to him, you had better be prepared to withstand significant scrutiny. "When you did a proposal," says Steve Schwartz, long-standing executive and director of the Wyss Medical Foundation, "he would become very critical about some part of it for the first couple minutes. And then you would work your way through that. Eventually, you could reach a point where now he's OK, he's mentally OK—he has bought into it. And then you could get what you want. But the first response was almost always a negative response, something like, 'This makes no sense. Why are we doing it this way?'"[17] Although such a skeptical response could be hard to take at first, employees who took the time to prepare usually came to appreciate and respect Wyss's rigorous thought process as well as the wise judgments it usually produced.

Wyss's habit of questioning everything has led to exciting opportunities in philanthropy (as explored throughout this book), allowing him to think big and maximize his impact—particularly in the creation of the Wyss Institute for Biologically Inspired Engineering at Harvard University. Wyss understood that scientists, as smart and productive as they are, often are holed up in academic silos, which impedes innovation. Instead, scientists need to work in an environment where they can't just pursue their little area of research—where they're challenged by others, where they have to spend time analyzing and evaluating other projects while other people evaluate their projects. Realizing that the divide between academia and business prevented new ideas from having an impact in the wider world, Wyss inspired the institute to combine the best of both worlds. The result was an academic institution unlike anything that existed in the United States or anywhere in the world.

Wyss's inclination to question everything also helped to spark his decades-long involvement in conservation. As an engineering student during the 1950s, Wyss and his classmates were charged with planning the construction of new highways running through his hometown of Bern. His classmates, who were applying strict engineering principles and abstract formulas, designed the highway in such a manner that it destroyed an entire forest near the city—a "horrendously bad" idea, in Wyss's view, that violated the dictates of common sense. Having noticed other instances in which conventional thinking prevailed at the expense of natural landscapes, Wyss developed early in his life a determination to do whatever he could to protect these vulnerable spaces. Even before he landed in Denver and developed a fascination with the American West, his critical bent put him on a path that would one day lead him to become perhaps the most impactful and effective conservationist in more than a century, protecting a hundred million acres of land and galvanizing the world around the goal of preserving 30 percent of Earth's land and water by 2030.

It is easy to proceed in standard or expected ways, missing opportunities that lurk right under our nose. As Wyss moves through the world, he can't help but imagine as-yet unrealized possibilities, nor can he help challenging himself and others to act on his insights. The result, during his years at Synthes and ever since, has been a restless dynamism—a willingness to take creative risks that may sometimes lead to miscues but also have allowed him to maximize his impact.

All of us can draw inspiration from Wyss's example. Whether we're planning a new social action campaign, hiring people for our organization, or plotting out our career, we can set aside our doubts, open up our minds, and become just a bit more imaginative about what might be. If you want to do a little bit of good, stick with the well-trodden path. If you want to truly change the world, get in the habit of constantly asking questions so you can develop keener insight. Then *act* on that insight, making moves that others might regard as crazy today, but that they'll later celebrate as breathtaking in their capacity to transform.

2

THE RIGHT REASON TO GO OUT OF BUSINESS

Put everything you've got into pursuing a socially beneficial mission, and you won't just make money—you'll make a difference.

IN 1983, AFTER TEN years spent working at Johnson & Johnson, Rick Gennett decided he'd had enough of the big corporate environment. Hoping to work for a smaller player in the medical devices field, he interviewed at Synthes, then an up-and-coming innovator with about $30 million in annual sales. The conversations seemed promising, but as the hiring process progressed, Gennett remained unconvinced about working there. He found it hard to get a sense of Synthes's culture from speaking to employees and managers.

During his final interview, Gennett met with the big boss, Hansjörg Wyss. This conversation, too, seemed to go well, but as the interview was wrapping up, Gennett still didn't feel especially drawn to the company. Then

Wyss made a casual comment that changed everything. Walking Gennett to the door, he said, "You know, we're not building this company to make money, so we'll probably go out of business. But we need to do the right things, and if we go out of business doing the right things, that's OK."[18]

Gennett was floored. The leaders he'd encountered at other companies had proudly touted their organizations' profitability. Although some had mentioned a social mission, it was clear that money was what really mattered. In contrast, Wyss not only prioritized Synthes's social purpose but proclaimed his willingness to forgo profits on its behalf. What kind of CEO took that stance? And what kind communicated it so openly and honestly in a job interview?

"I just had to work for this guy," Gennett says now. "The integrity was so palpable. In a capitalist system, everything is driven by money as the goal. And what he decided to do [instead] was to go after serving the customer—and if we did that right, they would buy more from us than we could ever sell them [otherwise]." [19]

Wyss's socially minded approach did indeed pay off—for everyone. Between 1987 and 1998, Synthes grew its sales of internal fixation implants from $64 million to $434 million.[20] Gennett took the job and stayed at Synthes for three decades, rising to become president of its core business, building plates and screws used to treat bone trauma. Over a sixteen-year period ending in 2010, he grew sales by nearly a factor of ten, from $185 million to $1.3 billion.[21]

Companies love to talk about how much good they're doing for society, and some really do practice what they preach. But many more use corporate purpose as a cover for what they *really* care about: profits. These companies are happy to do good—so long as they can also do well. When they can't make money (which turns out to be quite a bit of the time), well, the good stuff can wait.[22] No wonder public skepticism about companies is mounting.[23]

At Synthes, the social mission was to serve orthopedic surgeons—and by extension, patients—by providing surgeons with the highest-quality implants as well as the best technical expertise and training to support their success. Like the AO/ASIF doctors themselves, Wyss wanted to see a world in which surgeons everywhere would be equipped to help patients heal faster and more completely while experiencing fewer complications than with traditional immobilization techniques. Wyss didn't evangelize this mission on the company website, nor did he get up before large audiences to boast about how well the company was delivering on it. He didn't even formalize it as a mission statement to be framed and hung on the office walls. But inside the company, he and other senior leaders left little doubt about what mattered. Serving the customer came first; making money was second. If the customer was happy, financial rewards would come. And if for some reason they didn't, Wyss still wasn't about to compromise the purpose. Instead, he would let the company go under, taking solace in knowing that at least the company had pursued a higher purpose as best it could.

A BUILDER, NOT A MONEY GUY

You might find such an idealistic approach coming from the C-suite hard to believe, particularly when the person advocating for it eventually became a billionaire. But Wyss doesn't seem to have ever cared about wealth all that much. And to the extent he does, he cares *more* about how that wealth can create a positive and lasting impact. His attorney and confidant Christoph Megert captures Wyss's mindset well: "I think he is interested in achieving things he wants to achieve. But his achievement is not directed at earning a lot of money. It's nice to have, and it helps him to do things, but it's not wealth in itself that is a goal. The goal is to do something, to be successful in building. He is a builder."[24]

Debbie Davis, Wyss's former administrative assistant, has a similar impression. "What was inspiring to me," she says, "was that his purpose always was improving patient care. It wasn't the money. I mean, not that he didn't expect it to be profitable, but his main goal was to help people and to improve patient care with our products, which we did."[25]

As proof of Wyss's tendency to value meaning over money, consider his sheer willingness to give his fortune away. He is one of just a handful of the world's uberwealthy who have signed the Giving Pledge, a campaign urging donation of half their fortune to philanthropic causes. (As of 2023, only 241 people—less than 10 percent of the 2,640 people who ranked as billionaires that year—have done so.)[26] Talk to Wyss today, and you'll find him critical of wealthy people and their underdeveloped sense of civic responsibility. As he observes, wealthy people tend to feel terror at the prospect of losing their money. They love being wealthy—it's part of their identity—so they're constantly focused on maintaining and growing their riches. When they do contribute to social causes, they give only nominal amounts—not nearly enough to make a significant impact.

As Synthes grew during the 1990s and 2000s and became a public company, Wyss didn't run the business with an emphasis on short-term gains. "He never, from what I understood, was looking at the share price on the market," Megert remembers. "He was looking at the development of the company." Furthermore, during an era when CEO compensation was skyrocketing—including an increase of over 1,400 percent at large public companies between 1978 and 2021[27]—Wyss refrained from paying himself an exorbitant salary. "He was rather modest there," Megert continues. "He said, 'Well, I get dividends. I don't need more. That's good enough.'"[28]

Wyss also was notorious for denying himself and others the lavish perks that often come with leadership. "When I would rent a car for him," Davis remembers, "if it wasn't the cheapest car, he would be upset." Choosing to rent the least expensive cars meant they were sometimes so small that others felt uncomfortable riding in them. Debbie also remembers what one of the board members, who was a physically large man, once said to her: "'Don't put me in a small car with him again. It's impossible for me to get in and out of those cars.'"[29]

THE MAGIC OF THE VEPTR

It's one thing not to pine for wealth, but what does it mean to run a company that puts its social mission above its profits? For a glimpse into this approach, consider the case of a revolutionary device invented to treat a terrible affliction: thoracic insufficiency syndrome, or TIS—a rare, often fatal disorder affecting fewer than four thousand children in the United States each year.[30] Imagine what it must feel like to have a rib cage that, for structural reasons (such as the fusion of your ribs or the extreme curvature of your spine), is too small for your lungs to breathe normally. Every breath you take is a struggle, to the point where you can't participate in daily activities, and your lungs or heart eventually fail.

Pediatric orthopedic surgeons used to treat TIS by implanting rudimentary devices that attempted to straighten a child's spine and open up the chest cavity. Then, during the late 1980s, a surgeon by the name of Robert M. Campbell Jr. came up with an ingenious solution: a special artificial "rib" made of titanium implanted surgically in a child's body, which can be expanded periodically by the surgeon as the child grows.[31] But the VEPTR (vertical expandable prosthetic titanium rib), as this device is called, was a tough sell to device manufacturers. Campbell presented his drawings to several companies, but because the device was technically complex and the market for it was so small, they declined to make it.

One company said yes: Synthes. Some of the firm's leaders were inclined to turn Campbell away, just as their competitors had. In the short term, at least, Synthes would take a loss: After investing millions of dollars to manufacture the device, it wouldn't be able to generate sufficient sales. Wyss didn't disagree with this analysis, but he decided that the company would manufacture the product anyway. As he told the other leaders, "This is not a moneymaker. This will help children. So, we'll do it. And just you watch: We'll eventually get our money back a hundredfold."

Wyss was right. The company began producing the device in 1994 for use in clinical trials with kids. The US Food and Drug Administration granted humanitarian approval in 2004, and doctors soon began to use the device more broadly to treat severe early-onset scoliosis (curvature of the spine) in kids with critical, life-threatening deformities. To date, thousands of children around the world have benefited from lifesaving VEPTR devices. Although sales of the device were never meaningful for Synthes in financial terms, the device boosted the company's reputation. "It gave us a huge amount of credibility," Wyss says. "In this instance, unlike other companies, we had saved children. It was like buying advertising for the company. When you bring such a device to a surgeon in the children's part of a large hospital, and they suddenly have a device—word spreads throughout the whole hospital and helps you to sell your other products."

In 2019, the Wyss Medical Foundation gave $5 million to Children's Hospital of Philadelphia (CHOP) to establish the Wyss/Campbell Center for Thoracic Insufficiency Syndrome.[32] The center performs hundreds of surgeries each year, saving the lives of many children with this terrible condition.[33] Five years after the initial support to CHOP, Wyss pledged another $5 million.

SERVING SURGEONS (AND PATIENTS) FIRST

The most purpose-driven companies don't just dedicate a handful of products, programs, or initiatives to doing good; they instill the social mission at the very center of their business models and core operations. That's precisely what Wyss did at Synthes. Attending to the mission of serving surgeons—and ultimately, patients—became a powerful means of orienting the company in terms of both big, strategic moves and smaller, everyday decisions.

Under Wyss's direction, the company did everything possible to monitor and satisfy the needs of surgeons. Job number one was designing and manufacturing surgical devices that delivered significant value to surgeons and patients. As financier and former board member André

Mueller recalls, most Synthes board meeting agendas set aside time for the presentation of new products. Rather than focusing on how much money the company might make from a new product, however, the focus would be primarily on how the product would benefit surgeons and patients. "Very detailed questions were asked: What does it do for the surgeon? How does it improve the surgeon's work? What does it do for the patient? Will they get out of the hospital faster? Compared with, let's say, classical boards where it's all about the economics, [instead] it was a lot about products, about surgeon interaction."[34] It's not that Wyss didn't want to make money—he did. But as Mueller explains, the "accent was very much on product, on innovation," with Wyss assuming that the money would follow in due course.

Wyss also shined a spotlight on high standards. When Synthes decided to manufacture and sell a product, Wyss was adamant about achieving unequaled quality. "He had no time for something that wasn't perfect," says Steve Schwartz, long-standing executive and director of the Wyss Medical Foundation. "And he insisted that with any documentation, make sure you have attribution: who produced it, and when and what file it could be found in. He was absolutely insistent on that. He would be very upset if he saw something out of place. Inevitably, somebody would screw up, and [Wyss] would go crazy. Quality was the first thing."[35]

The emphasis on quality paid off. As former board member and prolific entrepreneur Amin J. Khoury notes, "The company's products were the gold standard, the best of the best. And the flow of new products was extraordinary."[36]

The availability of products also mattered. If a surgeon had a critically injured patient in need of an operation yet, for whatever reason, couldn't get the required surgical devices from Synthes, that was a big problem. To ensure that supply never failed to meet demand, Synthes's chief operating officer (COO)—the late Charlie Hedgepeth—personally monitored the number of back orders on a daily basis and posted that data on his wall. Every morning when Wyss was at company headquarters, he would join

Hedgepeth in reviewing the story told by the data. "Back orders kill your business and kill your reputation," explains Wyss, "because a surgeon says, 'How come I don't have this screw to fix this patient who just came in an hour ago?' So, we always looked at this."

When problems arose with back orders, Wyss took decisive action. Eric Lohrer, a former Synthes employee who currently helps Wyss manage his business investments, remembers a time when, soon after the company had made a major acquisition, the factories couldn't keep up with sales growth. "Hansjörg immediately instituted ways to increase production volumes," Lohrer says. "It wasn't a 'Can we afford to do this?' kind of situation. He just said, 'Look, we need to go and build more capacity. Figure out what it takes. If it's adding a fourth shift on the weekend, fine.' There was no hesitation, because [the delay] compromised customer service and patient care."[37]

It wasn't simply back orders. Any other problems that bore directly on the company's ability to serve surgeons prompted swift action on Wyss's part. He often broke through silos by just picking up the phone, striving to assemble just the right people to generate a solution. As Lohrer notes, Wyss had the latitude to do this, thanks to his ownership stake in the company, which eventually became a controlling one. It lent the company a nimble, entrepreneurial feel even after it had long ceased to be a small organization. "I think that focus on what really mattered for the success of the company, and his desire, willingness, and ability to immediately go find the solution, was critical to Synthes's success," Lohrer muses, summing up Wyss's perspective: "If you see something's wrong, go fix it."[38]

To ensure that surgeons were happy with the quality of Synthes products, and to identify ways the company might serve them even better, Wyss placed a premium on listening to them. As Khoury remembers, Wyss "had a wonderful penchant for spending lots of time with the surgeons, and he was really terrific at understanding what they thought might help to develop specific new products."[39]

It's a simple concept—listen to your customer—but large companies often fail to do it. To stay informed, Wyss personally maintained relationships with dozens, even hundreds of surgeons. One of them, Dr. Robert Teitge, now emeritus professor of orthopaedic surgery at Wayne State University in Michigan, remembers that Wyss "always showed immense respect for the surgeons and was intensely interested in their opinions, but never ever have I seen him suggest products. He was also always generous, not in the sense of putting on elaborate dinners or resort events for peddling his products, but with research and educational grants, and being genuinely interested in the well-being of the surgeons." Teitge also remembers that Wyss was uniquely equipped to comprehend surgeons' needs, explaining, "He's extremely curious about everything. He's very knowledgeable, he's very bright, he picks up things in a hurry, and he has a tremendous memory for details."[40]

When surgeons identified problems that were bedeviling them, including with Synthes's existing projects, Wyss would engage them in a collaborative effort to develop new and better products. At one point, Teitge disclosed to Wyss that the company's treatments for ligaments weren't that great and that an opportunity existed to improve them.

"Great. Let's develop something," Wyss suggested (as Teitge recalls). "I'll put you in contact with one of our engineers in product development." They worked with this engineer, and according to Teitge, "that's the way many new products came along."[41] Doctors also participated on technical committees convened by the AO Foundation to attack specific problems, working in turn with Synthes engineers to develop solutions. Although Wyss didn't quite have the bandwidth to participate, he kept abreast of the committees' ongoing work and continued to emphasize its importance.

In addition to working with surgeons, Wyss also spent a good deal of time interacting with frontline sales consultants to understand their first-hand impressions of the market. Synthes sales consultants truly were in the trenches, perhaps more so than their counterparts in other industries. They didn't simply quote and negotiate prices or make sales pitches; they functioned in the first instance as technical experts. Surgeons and members of their teams consulted the Synthes consultants on a daily or weekly basis when planning out highly specialized surgical procedures, to make sure that they were using the right devices in the right way and that they could access the necessary devices and tools. A consultant might even be present in the operating room to offer advice during a procedure. If anyone knew what surgeons needed from Synthes so they could offer the best patient care, the sales consultants did. Realizing this, Wyss made it his business to spend time with them and urged other leaders to take their feedback seriously.

Regular interaction with the sales force positioned Wyss to inspire young consultants (and in the case of new products, product development engineers) and teach them how best to listen to surgeons. Lacking experience, these company representatives sometimes met with surgeons but didn't really listen to them. When a surgeon made a point, instead of fully registering it and making a note of it, the new Synthes representative would offer a counterargument, seeking to prove the surgeon wrong.

"I was with Wyss on several occasions when he would directly overrule the Synthes employee," Schwartz says, recalling that Wyss would direct the employee to "let the surgeon tell their story and be fully heard."[42] Wyss also demanded that sales consultants take down verbatim what surgeons said rather than rely on their memory of conversations. Surgeons needed to control the conversation, and sales consultants needed to pay attention—not just because of the valuable customer information that approach yielded but because of the respect that Wyss felt the company (and he personally) owed them.

A DIFFERENT KIND OF SALES FORCE

The quality of the sales force was fundamental to Wyss's ambition of catering closely to surgeons' needs. "The Synthes sales force was somewhat unique in never suggesting or selling a product," Professor Teitge remembers. “Competitors’ sales forces would attempt to push their products on the OR [operating room] directors, but this was the opposite of the Synthes sales force, which just provided the OR with whatever had been requested but did not suggest or push a product.”[43]

Synthes sales consultants had to be highly motivated and dedicated to satisfying their customers, even more so than their peers at competing companies. Patients schedule hip and knee replacements well in advance and usually during working hours, which means that the sales consultants at other companies that deal with those products enjoy a predictable life. By contrast, fractures tend to be more complex, and when they occur, it is usually due to an accident or some other emergency. So, Synthes sales consultants were prepared to receive a phone call at any time from a surgeon asking for their help—even nights and weekends.

That was the ethic at Synthes: *Do whatever it takes to deliver on the mission.* As Steve Schwartz remembers, “It didn’t matter how late you’d have to stay in the office or if you’re working on weekends or something. If there’s something that we needed to get done to help a surgeon, we got it done.” Because of this “all-hands-on-deck mentality,” Schwartz felt that some employees tended to think of Synthes as an “overgrown start-up because we ran it like a start-up.”[44]

To give surgeons the support they needed, the company ensured that sales consultants received extraordinary levels of technical training. When new consultants joined the company, they underwent four to six weeks of courses to understand the specifics of Synthes products and the nuances of how surgeons used those products in patients. Consultants also visited a manufacturing plant, toured the factory floor, and helped make a sample item.

“It was very, very thorough,” Lohrer remembers—more so than what competitors provided. The model for such training was the courses in internal fixation techniques that the AO/ASIF (the nonprofit research and teaching organization attached to Synthes) had offered surgeons themselves starting in the 1960s. “The level of depth in that training, the thought and passion that went into it, in my opinion, also became part of the DNA of Synthes," Lohrer explains. "The idea was for you as a sales rep or manager to be proud that you or your people were the best trained in the hospital."[45]

Because they were so well trained, Synthes sales consultants could accompany surgeons to their own trainings and help new surgeons learn how to work with the company's implants. This knowledge transfer helped the younger surgeons and their patients, and it also was extremely effective as a sales technique, since sales consultants had an opportunity to experience valuable face time with these surgeons away from the demands of the hospital.

Other companies offered surgeons a chance to train on their products, but it wasn't the same, in part because the sales consultants who assisted with the training weren't as knowledgeable as Synthes consultants. Lohrer recalls seeing product managers from other companies who, even after eighteen months on the job, couldn't remember steps in specific surgeries. At Synthes, that would have been unacceptable. "You wouldn't necessarily have been fired right away, but you would have gotten into a lot of trouble. This is your baby. You need to know it inside and out," Lohrer says. "It's just a different level of quality in the training of people."[46]

TUNE OUT THE BULLSHIT

Well-intentioned companies can become sidetracked with aspects of the business that sound important but don't really help deliver on the mission. Wyss was determined to avoid this trap, and by all accounts, he did. To maintain a focus on surgeons and their needs, he deprioritized everything else. Revenues mattered: They reflected the value that surgeons placed on Synthes's products. Other metrics like net profit and cost control didn't matter as much, so they received less focus. The human resources department didn't bear directly on serving surgeons, so although Synthes had one, Wyss kept it to a minimum. Marketing in the conventional sense was practically nonexistent at the company—what mattered, again, was the sales force's provision of high-quality expertise.

"Messaging—how do I position the product, what is the pricing strategy—none of that was done at Synthes," Lohrer says. "It was all about happy customers who then would use the product."[47]

As Wyss notes, the company was so focused on its mission that it stopped joining peer companies at industry conferences. In part, that decision reflected Wyss's desire to keep Synthes's success out of the limelight. The big orthopedic device companies concentrated on hip and knee replacements, which were more profitable than Synthes's core business of providing plates and screws to fix trauma-damaged bones in the body. But the trauma business was still quite profitable, and while the industry's gaze was directed elsewhere, Synthes snagged a big percentage of that market. If the bigger players understood what a good business Synthes had built and how they'd built it, they'd want to jump in and compete more aggressively, crimping Synthes's margins and market share. Keeping it quiet made good strategic sense.

But as Wyss also realized, attending industry conferences didn't do much to help with the core mission of serving surgeons. "I hate nonconstructive meetings," Wyss says, and conferences were essentially useless. "It didn't bring any advantage. You go to a meeting of a professional organization with your competitors. Yeah, it's nice; you have a really nice lunch or a wonderful dinner, and there is bullshit talk all afternoon, but nothing happens. We didn't need industry associations to do a good job." For a similar reason, the company paused all advertising when Wyss took over in 1977. It just didn't help Synthes's mission, so it wasn't worth doing.

One reason Synthes could afford to minimize attendance at industry conferences was that it had a much better way of making connections with surgeons and teaching them about their products: Continuing Medical Education trainings run by the AO Foundation. Widely regarded as the best in the industry, these trainings were peer taught, with well-respected surgeons sharing valuable knowledge and techniques that their counterparts wouldn't necessarily learn during medical school or residency. As Wyss notes, the point of the trainings was "not to sell instruments." Instead, they were designed to be "learning experiences for doctors." Of course, in the process of learning to perform procedures with cadaver or plastic bones, doctors would have a chance to work with Synthes products and discover their superior quality for themselves. The doctors would then request that their hospitals buy and use these products without Synthes having to directly sell them on it.

Wyss and other leaders could sometimes take the discipline of Synthes's core mission too far, at the expense of recognizing a valuable innovation. One year, Rick Gennett, as president of Synthes Trauma, proposed to the board that the company install inventory management systems in as many hospitals as possible. Nurses on surgical teams sometimes overstocked key Synthes products to make sure that they didn't run out. As a result, hospitals often wound up with inventory they didn't need. After a while, they sought to return unused products to Synthes for a credit on their account. Gennett's idea was to provide hospitals with a cabinet to store Synthes products as well as a scanner and a laptop computer fixed to the cabinet. Nurses would scan products when stocking the cabinet and using products. The system would monitor stock levels and automatically place orders at Synthes when stock was running low.

To Gennett, this system was an obvious improvement. As hospitals returned overstocked products to Synthes, the company could sometimes have too much inventory on hand. This could disrupt the sales cycle: Once the company credited a hospital for the returned product, Synthes wouldn't be earning any new revenue until the credits ran down. Providing an inventory management system would not only solve these problems but also serve as a barrier to competition. With these systems in place, it would be easier for hospitals to order from Synthes than from other companies. Most important, an inventory management system would help operating room staff by making it easier for them to find the products they needed when performing procedures and would prevent their hospital from running out.

Given that such a system would directly support Synthes's mission while also delivering other benefits, Gennett assumed that Wyss and others on the board would authorize a budget and allow him to proceed. He was wrong. Not seeing the connection with the mission as strongly as Gennett did, they dismissed inventory management as a diversion that offered little value. Undeterred, Gennett refined his pitch and, three months later, presented the idea again. It was again rejected.

At this point, Gennett did something that might have gotten him fired at another company: He went ahead with the initiative anyway. Using money in a discretionary fund, he instructed his team to design and build the Synthes Inventory Management System, or SIMS, and begin installing it in hospitals. He told his people not to discuss SIMS inside the company. But SIMS soon proved to be a tremendous success: Within six to seven years, 95 percent of all trauma sales were coming into Synthes through SIMS. By this time, board members not only knew about SIMS—they seemed to have remembered sanctioning it originally, even though they hadn't. And that was perfectly fine with Gennett.

Even the best mission-focused leaders can't get every decision right. In his zeal to avoid distractions, Wyss might have failed to grasp fully the opportunity that SIMS represented to serve surgeons better. What's even more revealing, however, is Gennett's willingness to pursue the project anyway. After all, wasn't he worried that Wyss would become angry upon discovering that Gennett hadn't respected the board's decision? "I think he would have been more likely to give me credit for persevering," Gennett says. "After all, it would have compromised patient care if doctors couldn't find what they need."[48]

It's hard for leaders to weave a deep respect for the mission into an organization's culture. But Wyss had done so, to the point where well-intentioned people inside the firm were willing to take the initiative on behalf of the mission, knowing that they need not fear punishment for it.

To maximize our impact, we can't just believe abstractly in a higher purpose. We must put purpose at the very center of the business model, caring more about our mission than we do about making money or achieving some other gain. Given how complex and stressful the world is, it can be hard to get our priorities straight and even harder to remain on the right path over time. But we can hope to make meaningful, lasting change only if we know what matters most and focus relentlessly and unapologetically on that purpose.

3

THE PROBLEM WITH HOTEL BUFFETS

Pursue change by using your greatest intellectual assets, which are also the most basic: common sense and simple pragmatism.

THERE'S A STORY SYNTHES people like to tell, and it has to do with bananas. The company was scheduling a meeting at a resort hotel run by a major chain, and Hansjörg Wyss made a special request: He wanted the hotel to serve whole bananas at the breakfast buffet rather than cut fruit. Some people find cut fruit delightful—no need to bother with a messy peel so early in the morning—but to Wyss, it was unconscionable.

At hotel buffets, guests never fully consume the massive amounts of food on offer. They don't even eat a small fraction of it. The leftovers—great mounds of them—are thrown out. Wyss cringed at such unnecessary waste. He couldn't prevent the resort from serving a breakfast buffet—that's what they offered. But he could at least minimize the damage. By serving whole bananas, the resort would be able to use any uneaten ones at its next event.

Event coordinators at the resort either didn't get Wyss's request or decided to ignore it. Whatever the case, when Wyss and the other company executives showed up, they found cut fruit. Furious, Wyss proclaimed that from then on, the company wouldn't book any more events with that hotel chain. He was done with them. As for Synthes executives, they got a good laugh. The episode went down in Synthes lore as a classic Hansjörg Wyss story, one that invariably called to mind the old 1920s song "Yes! We Have No Bananas."

Wastefulness of any kind has been one of Wyss's greatest pet peeves as a leader. While on a business trip to Switzerland, one Synthes executive unleashed a firestorm by casually mentioning to Wyss that he had been booked (without his knowledge) into a very expensive luxury hotel. Wyss demanded that he check out right then and there and find a room at the local Ramada Inn instead. The executive promptly did that, and good thing: The next day Wyss called to confirm that the hotel had in fact been changed. Another former Synthes executive remembers a time before a business meeting when he stood in a prime paid parking spot to save it for Wyss. But rather than take the spot, Wyss drove around for fifteen or twenty minutes, eventually finding street parking, which was free. He was quite proud that he had been able to save a couple of dollars.

Caring about such small savings might seem petty, but Wyss saw a bigger picture. As longtime Synthes executive Rick Gennett relates, health care during the 1980s and 1990s was a relatively easy industry to operate in. The hospitals and doctors buying from companies like Synthes weren't the ones to ultimately pay for the products; insurance companies did. As a result, there was greater tolerance for higher prices, because hospitals and doctors could just pass the expense on to insurance companies, which in turn passed it on to their customers.[49] But Wyss realized that one day this would change. To prepare for this eventuality, the company had to cultivate frugal financial habits—it couldn't afford to retain needless fat in the organization. And Wyss felt strongly that he had to model frugality personally. If people saw him wasting money, they'd feel free to do so themselves. The next thing you knew, the company's costs would soar.

Wyss's concern about waste was about saving not just money but also time. As explained in the previous chapter, he detests the long, pointless meetings that clog up the works at so many organizations. As a result, he did everything he could to banish them from Synthes. At meetings, he wouldn't hesitate to intercede if he perceived that a speaker was rambling on and wasting everyone's time. "I was rude," he admits with some measure of regret.

During one ongoing series of important meetings, a senior leader kicked off the proceedings each time by providing the same ten-minute introduction to the subject at hand. The third or fourth time this happened, Wyss couldn't contain himself. He took the leader to task, exclaiming, "You've told us this same crap already. We all know why we're here. Tell us something substantial." Wyss recalls that people chafed against his direct style, but "in this instance, I didn't care because I wanted a substantive discussion about the opportunity at hand, and we were wasting time."

Wyss's objection is not about using up resources per se—it's about doing so irresponsibly, in ways that don't yield real benefit. He notes that wealthy people often spend obscenely, simply because they can. A billionaire might fly on a whim down to the South Pole to spend a night glamping out on the ice before flying home in the morning. Wyss shakes his head at such blatant extravagance. It would be one thing to travel to the South Pole for educational or scientific purposes—to learn something about the historic expeditions of explorers like Ernest Shackleton, for instance, or to study the changes wrought by the climate crisis. But going for a single night, for no real purpose, doesn't do anyone any good—it's wasteful.

Wyss sees wealth as affording a pathway to personal fulfillment: You have resources to pursue serious interests and hobbies that enrich your life. Money also enables you to help people—in your social circle, your community, your country, or the wider world. But spending thoughtlessly or out of vanity or as a way of wielding power over others—that's immoral, especially when most people around the world have so little.

SHAKING UP THE FACTORY

Wyss's frugality points us to a broader tendency of his, one that has been key to his outsized impact: his pragmatic mindset. Profligacy, in his view, isn't just immoral or irresponsible; it also *makes no sense.* Being wasteful means one is ignoring or misunderstanding the practical function that resources serve in our lives. These resources are valuable and scarce. Common sense says to respect their value and use them wisely.

At Synthes and later at his foundation, Wyss's pragmatism led him not just to avoid lavish spending but to place a strong emphasis on efficient processes and controls, most notably when it came to manufacturing. When Wyss took over as Synthes CEO in 1977, one of his early moves was to establish a production facility in Colorado to provide for the US market. As the company expanded and became global, he added other facilities in the United States and elsewhere—thirteen in total by the early 2010s.[50] Traditionally, American companies focused on manufacturing their products in bulk and maintaining large inventories. The idea was to keep enough on hand so the company could service any demand it might see—a strategy called "just in case."[51] The downsides were that companies had to warehouse these finished products, which represented an added expense, and that they couldn't respond quickly to shifts in the market.

By chance, Wyss happened to meet a Japanese manufacturing consultant named Kei Abe who was well versed in a different production approach called "just in time," otherwise known as the Toyota Production System.[52] This approach organizes production lines so that machines make smaller runs of specific products, switching quickly between outputs as needed to meet customer demand (hence "just in time"): A machine that manufactures one part on Monday might be quickly reset to make a different part on Tuesday. With just-in-time manufacturing, companies don't have to keep large stockpiles of finished goods, hoping customers will show up to buy them. They also don't have to keep large quantities of raw materials on hand—they can order those "just in time" from their suppliers as well. Just-in-time is far more efficient, and it allows factories to be far more responsive to shifts in the market.

Starting around 1990—well ahead of the rest of the industry—Wyss brought in Abe to redesign production at Synthes's main plant in Colorado. The process of changing to just-in-time manufacturing took about two years and required a wholesale transformation of the factory floor. At first, Synthes workers and engineers resisted the changes, not least because of the way Abe went about implementing them. He was abrasive, a "disruptive presence," Wyss remembers. "He might meet with engineers for a couple of days, and the engineers didn't understand what he was saying, and he would say, 'Dumb! Dumb Americans!' I had to go in and calm everybody down afterward."

Wyss persisted with the changes, however, transforming the Colorado facility and designing others to look exactly like a world-class Japanese factory. Within a few years, Synthes saw enormous improvements in efficiency. As the first in its industry to implement just-in-time production, the company became the lowest-cost manufacturer, realizing margins that were 15 percent to 20 percent better than those of competitors making similar products. Resistance on the factory floor subsided as employees and managers saw not only the positive results but also the impact on workers' jobs.

To achieve greater efficiencies, the just-in-time system devolved more authority to Synthes workers. Individual machinists received sales figures midway through the typical workweek and then had the power to plan their own production schedules to meet demand. Workers helped engineers design processes for reconfiguring machines to make rapid shifts between production runs of different goods.

Synthes workers also gained more responsibility over quality. At traditional factories, quality inspectors might scrutinize production lines, stopping production when they spot a defect. With just-in-time, Synthes machinists monitored their own production and had the power to halt production when necessary. Managers still performed quality inspections at the end of the manufacturing process, but workers played the key role. All this added responsibility meant that workers became more highly skilled and commanded higher pay, while their daily work became more interesting and intellectually challenging.

PRACTICING ENLIGHTENED PRAGMATISM

Pragmatism for Wyss was never just about making more money or even achieving more social good. It was also about running a business that benefited workers. As he saw it, workers were "the backbone of the company," doing the actual work of production while gaining vital frontline knowledge. The company couldn't thrive unless its workers felt happy, respected, and well treated. Implementing key policies such as just-in-time manufacturing would have been counterproductive for the company had it not simultaneously improved workers' job satisfaction.

Beyond practical considerations, Wyss regards caring for workers as a moral imperative, one that must always temper and inform the imperatives of frugality and efficiency. In his view, capitalism all too often pursues efficiency and profits at the expense of workers' welfare. He points to factory conditions in England during the late eighteenth century as a prime example of this, and he faults the Enlightenment-era economist Adam Smith for being oblivious to the deficits in his influential philosophy. Smith, he argues, "didn't care at all how the people lived in the English factory towns. He didn't give a shit. Those towns are horrible." Further, thanks to predatory lending practices, "the employees couldn't ever change jobs. They were totally tied down in chains by the company." Too many modern companies operate in a similar fashion, Wyss believes, putting profits far ahead of the people who help create them.

By contrast, Wyss felt a personal sense of responsibility to see to workers' welfare. "An ethical executive really worries about the well-being of the lowest-paid person in the company or the person with the least amount of responsibility," Wyss says. "Even the janitor has to have a good health-care plan in a large company that's successful. And that's the responsibility of the CEO. The company must have a system where nobody would lose [their] house because of medical bills."

Wyss today looks back with pride on how Synthes treated its line workers. Machinists at its plants were some of the best paid in the industry, receiving profit-sharing payments every year in addition to high levels of hourly compensation. Further, their compensation was more fairly pegged to that of managers in the upper echelons than at other firms. CEOs at large firms today can make five hundred times or more what line workers make. To Wyss, that's a disgrace. For many years at Synthes, even as the company experienced stratospheric growth, he kept his own salary fixed. Given that he owned much of the company, Wyss was confident that one day he would reap significant value if he sold his stake. He eventually did just that, but only after many years of adhering to the principles he felt strongly about: treating workers fairly and avoiding obscene salary gaps.

MASTERING THE DETAILS FROM THE GROUND UP

Although it has been over a decade since Wyss led Synthes and almost three decades since he implemented just-in-time manufacturing, he still speaks of company policies with both genuine delight and a keen command of the details. That's no accident. Central to his pragmatic mindset was—and is—the idea that you can only succeed with a project if you understand it in detail from the ground up.

To run a business, you can't rely on the abstractions they teach you in business school, nor can you take the word of high-priced consultants, subject-matter experts, or midlevel managers. The business can't exist merely as a concept in your mind. You must gain a firsthand understanding of production, sales processes, and market conditions. You must experience the business directly and retain a sense of it as a living, breathing organism. That's the only way to gain the practical insight required to make smart, workable decisions rooted in common sense.

From the beginning of his career, Wyss made it a central practice of his job to obtain a complete and detailed picture of business operations. Before Synthes, when he served as managing director of the Swedish textile company, Wyss was tasked with turning around that struggling enterprise. Despite starting with very little knowledge about making women's dresses, he familiarized himself with the business and the industry not by relying on what other executives told him or consulting fashion experts but by immersing himself in the basics of the business. As he related in a published business school case study, "[I] conducted a detailed and systematic investigation of all aspects of company operations. Given the uneven attention paid by my predecessor to the different segments of the company, I was particularly anxious to focus on all areas."[53]

Although Wyss didn't speak Swedish, he visited the manufacturing plant and spoke with people on the ground as best he could. He asked many questions, inviting people to explain their jobs to him. "In my questioning, I usually try to get into details," he points out. "Only in this way do you really find out what is going on and build a platform for future action." Not knowing Swedish, Wyss had no choice but to delegate, but he maintained an open-door policy with the plant managers, consulting with them on a near-daily basis: "Usually, our meetings [lasted] between thirty minutes and one hour, and they almost always [related] to a specific operating problem."[54]

Wyss's approach paid off. When he first arrived at the company, it was losing money; a year later the company was projecting a "decent profit," thanks to changes he instituted.

"I think that we have rescued [the company]," he remarked at the time, "and all our attention up to this point was focused on this task." Top managers at the organization were very happy with his leadership. One of them reported feeling "several years younger" after Wyss arrived. Another expressed happiness at Wyss's dedicated presence in the plant and willingness to meet with him often as issues arose.[55]

Wyss later applied this same hands-on, details-oriented approach to find success at Synthes. When he first joined the company, he spent months learning about orthopedic surgery and technical aspects of the company's products as well as its operations. According to Gennett, "He engaged in deep technical conversations with surgeons, especially early. He wanted to understand as much as he could from what the surgeon was saying. He wanted to know what their challenges were from a product development standpoint—with hundreds of surgeons."[56]

Once Wyss had manufacturing operations up and running, he made a practice of staying in regular touch with frontline workers—something he continued to do as the company grew. When he visited Synthes's factories, he would tell the plant manager that meeting with them wasn't his only priority. Rather, he wanted to spend time one-on-one with long-term employees working the machines. During these encounters, which lasted for the first hour or so of each visit, he would ask about their personal lives, their work, and the changes they had seen. Only then would he go to the conference room for the plant manager's presentation of the facility's latest performance numbers.

According to Wyss's friend and former companion Marcey Olajos, "He was a leader who would go down on the manufacturing floor and know the guys' names that were working. [He] understood what they were doing—could ask them questions, listen to their problems. He never sat up in an office in the ivory tower and tried to run things from there. He was somebody who made sure he knew the people doing the work. He wanted to know how things were run."[57]

Wyss visited each of the company's widely dispersed manufacturing facilities—in Colorado, New York, Pennsylvania, and elsewhere—once every six weeks or so, and traveled to facilities closer to the company's headquarters on a weekly basis. He wanted to get beyond the output numbers he was seeing to understand operations on a qualitative level—the problems that were arising, the state of morale, the kinds of daily decisions managers were making. Sometimes the insights he uncovered were small; sometimes they were much larger. On one occasion, while visiting the Colorado factory about eighteen months after it had implemented just-in-time manufacturing, Wyss learned that a new vice president of manufacturing was reversing all the positive changes the plant had just made. This leader simply didn't get the approach or what Wyss was trying to accomplish. Wyss wound up replacing him. Had he not been on-site to uncover the problem quickly, it might have festered, leading to disarray at the plant.

Wyss maintained close contact with the sales team as well. "He would talk to any employee for any length of time," Rick Gennett recalls, "and he found it genuinely fascinating: what they were up to, what they were working on, what their opinion was about something he was trying to decide about. He got a wide range of opinions about every major decision. He would always ask people in (and outside) the organization their feelings on the subject."[58]

Wyss sometimes met with sales consultants on his own, without Gennett present. He would listen to their feedback and then ask Gennett to improve certain policies based on what he'd heard. "He would never dictate," Gennett says. "He might ask a question, or he might say, 'I know you're right, but do this anyway, just for them.' He would always try to please [the sales consultants] and support them. And he gained a lot of wisdom that way. He was hearing directly from the field what was happening in the company, what the people on the front lines saw that we were doing right or wrong."[59]

Wyss's interest in and reliance on contact with frontline workers made him allergic to bureaucratic processes that stood in the way of real conversations and learning. In detesting performance reviews—a stance that he maintains to this day—Wyss was ahead of his time. Parsing his thinking, Wyss Foundation president Molly McUsic says, "If you don't [already] know how the people reporting to you are doing, and [if] they don't know how you think about them all year long, you've failed." In general, McUsic observes, Wyss advises business leaders to "get rid of as many bureaucratic systems as you can, so that the organization is flexible and spry."[60]

Wyss's engaged, consultative style as a leader didn't mean he ran Synthes as a democracy. Although he listened carefully, he didn't hesitate to act once he felt he understood a topic well enough, nor did he feel compelled to agree with what he'd heard. One year, Synthes dispensed with traditional business attire (as described in the next chapter) and adopted a more casual dress code, a measure that helped to close the psychological gap between leaders and line workers. In coming to this decision, Wyss held a meeting of the company's vice presidents and went around the room, asking them all to weigh in. To a person, the vice presidents all advised that the company should adopt business casual on Fridays only, as "that was the way big companies in New York were doing it," he recalls.

But deference to New York companies or any other external authority didn't hold much weight with Wyss. He was, as always, focused on a practical problem. At the company's headquarters, which comprised both a machine shop and executive offices, seeing such a stark difference in how white- and blue-collar employees dressed—one in suit and tie, the other in blue overalls—was awkward and culturally corrosive. Wyss's common sense told him that changing to casual dress wouldn't impact performance—that executives "didn't think better when they're wearing a tie."

"OK, thank you for your input," he said to the other leaders assembled. "I appreciate it. We're going to business casual all the time." Wyss was an approachable boss who listened to input, but there was never any doubt that he was firmly in charge. Having consulted others, he trusted his own instincts and understanding of what the situation required above all.

Many well-intended initiatives falter because the people leading them lack common sense. We might want to have an impact, but we become too distant, wasting resources and making foolish, poorly informed decisions. To maximize the good we do, we can cultivate a more practical mindset.

We can become more conscious of our spending, even if our budgets aren't pinched. We can become as efficient as possible in what we do.

As our organization grows or our career takes off, we can stay as close as possible to the *real* work, peeling away layers of bureaucracy if need be. We can understand the details and make even minor decisions in a thoughtful, informed way. It might seem that something as small as bananas at a breakfast buffet doesn't matter. But as Wyss teaches us, it often does.

4

THIS CEO DRIVES A SUBARU

Wield greater influence by connecting on a human level, leaving pretension behind, and refusing to hold yourself above others.

WYSS WAS UNYIELDING WHEN it came to the quality of Synthes products and uncompromising when offering surgeons the very best technical support. He drove the company hard to operate efficiently with a minimum of waste. But he wasn't boring or an old fuddy-duddy—not by any means. His robust sense of humor and taste for fun are qualities that endeared him to people across the organization. At one of the company's annual sales meetings, Wyss regaled hundreds of sales consultants in attendance by dressing up and speaking like Yoda from *Star Wars*. "As you can imagine," Lohrer says, "if you do that kind of stuff—showing everybody that you're not above some self-deprecating humor, I mean—they love you. People absolutely adored the guy."[61]

Wyss could be very tough with people when he perceived that they were trying to offer him ideas that weren't fully considered. He could complain loudly when something was not to his liking. But people overlooked this behavior because his heart was clearly in the right place and, just as important, because he just didn't take himself too seriously. Compared with other CEOs, Wyss seemed strikingly unpretentious—in terms of not just his sense of humor but his attire, personal habits, and consumer choices. "He would just drive up in his old Subaru," Lohrer says. "And people are like, 'Wait, isn't the guy rich?' And he's like, 'I don't care.' Or he would show up in normal clothes. If you didn't know who he was, you absolutely would not pick him out of the line."[62]

Lohrer remembers an incident during the mid-2000s when Wyss made a surprise visit to a recently finished (but still largely empty) building that the company had put up to house its spine business. Synthes was already a public company by then, and Wyss—who had stepped down as CEO but remained as chairman—was both very wealthy and legendary within the company. Yet he was unfamiliar with the new building, which is probably why two administrative assistants remarked that he looked lost and offered to help him. Wyss chatted with them for a few minutes and soon realized that they had no clue who he was. Unbothered by the lack of recognition, he went on his way without revealing his identity. Only then did Lohrer, who was sitting nearby, reveal to the assistants that they had been speaking to the company's erstwhile owner and CEO.

"They basically fell over backward," he says. "There was no minder with a suitcase, no fancy suit, nothing. That's the kind of guy he is."[63]

DON'T ACT LIKE A BOSS

It is often presumed that to command respect from others, leaders and professionals must adopt a certain formality and must closely guard perceptions about their status. Their authority, according to conventional wisdom, comes from their ability to seem different, better, privileged, more powerful than others around them. As Wyss intuitively understood, the opposite is true. Posturing and a sense of self-importance create distance and alienate people. Professionals—and leaders especially—can wield *more* influence by being themselves and connecting with others in a genuine way, as a human being. Because Wyss behaved more authentically than leaders typically do, others knew him better as a person and felt more comfortable expressing themselves in return. As Rick Gennett suggests, sales associates tended to speak freely with Wyss because "he never acted like the boss."[64]

This sense of intimacy led to an unusual amount of affection and loyalty for Wyss inside Synthes. Although naturally there were exceptions, most people loved working for him and loved the culture that he'd built. Rather than finding him overbearing, they admired him and sought constantly to win his approval. Wyss's administrative assistant Debbie Davis, who first started at the company in 1993—well before it became a global, publicly traded company—says, "In the years I was there, it was rare for anyone to leave Synthes. People loved working there."[65] The company's success made it an attractive place to work, of course, but it wasn't just that. Having a leader who was both inspiring and approachable mattered, too.

Wyss's authenticity as a leader was most palpable—sometimes humorously so—to those who worked closest with him. Steve Schwartz recounts what happened when, as a Synthes executive, he accompanied Wyss on a hiking trip. Members of the group were shimmying up a tight vertical passageway between rocks, one at a time, wedging their rear end against one side of the passageway to hold themselves steady while pulling upward with their arms and legs. "It was like a little line of people working their way up, and I'm right below Wyss," Schwartz says. "And I have my nose right near his rear end. I mean, it just looked weird."[66]

True to form, Wyss proceeded to joke with him, saying, "This is where you belong, Schwartz."

Wyss said something else interesting that day, referencing one of the company's main competitors: "You're never going to see the president of Stryker doing something like this." That was true—and not just because Wyss was much more of an athlete and outdoor enthusiast than the typical corporate leader, even into his eighties. He was also much more comfortable than most CEOs just being himself around the employees—and he was proud of that attribute. In his heart, he felt a basic sense of kinship with others around him, regardless of their role or position within the company. As he saw it, his identity as CEO was a relatively superficial one. More fundamentally, he was just an ordinary guy like anybody else. The impact on Schwartz and other close colleagues was electric.

Wyss's sense of himself as an ordinary guy was rooted in his humble upbringing, but not from any sense of deprivation per se. As he clarifies, he always had enough money while growing up to satisfy his wants and needs. Even on a limited budget, his parents managed to expose young Hansjörg to some of the more elevated things in life, such as music and art; his father was a skilled artist who took his son to museums and made small drawings for Wyss's mother. However, to get the spending money he needed, Wyss was forced to scrap around more than some of the other kids, working a series of odd jobs to earn extra cash. Even as a student at Harvard Business School, he had a side gig writing freelance articles for a prominent Swiss newspaper. It was another one of his talents: He had been writing for this paper for several years, first as a ski reporter and later as a correspondent covering American culture.

Being an ordinary guy was not without complications for Wyss, clashing as it did with his deeply held belief in his own intelligence and potential. Despite great reverence for how he was raised and the principles that informed his upbringing, he would never have been satisfied living an ordinary life in Bern, where he grew up. He saw through the provincialism of his small Swiss city and was motivated to grow beyond it.

What's more, he knew he was *capable* of growing beyond it—a fact affirmed by the decent grades he received in school when he applied himself. This sense of his own capabilities left Wyss feeling, on some level, that he had something to prove. During his youth, whenever others perceived themselves as his betters or disparaged him, Wyss took comfort in believing that they had it wrong—that one day they would be working for *him.* He had come from limited means but, unlike some, knew he wouldn't stay there for long. He was a common man, in his mind, but quite *un*common as well.

Regardless of this complexity, Wyss's casual demeanor and wide-ranging knowledge have allowed him to connect with a broad range of people—and not just within Synthes. "Hansjörg is a worldly man," Schwartz says. "So if you sit down and talk with him, the chances are you're going to connect on some topic that will leave you—whoever you are, if you're the clerk at the office or the chief of surgery at some academic center—[with] a connection of some type. And that's something I kind of learned from Hansjörg: the importance of being able to engage people on a variety of different levels, on a variety of different subjects."[67]

Wyss's late wife, the family therapist and best-selling author Rosamund Zander, once related that outside of work, Wyss maintains friendships with people from diverse walks of life who happen to share his interests. Zander cited a friendship he formed during the mid-2010s with a woman in Maine who, for decades, had worked alongside her husband to maintain an elaborate model train exhibit in a secluded barn. Wyss loves model trains—they are a longtime hobby of his, and he owns several just for the fun of it. Chatting with the woman, he discovered that she was struggling financially to pay for her train's upkeep, so he pledged to help her with that. He has kept in touch with her ever since, stopping in to see her when he's nearby.

"It's a down-to-earth thing," Zander explained. "He likes to be with people who don't have a lot of money and who live a down-to-earth life. The train is an opening to a relationship, but he's not bonding with her because of that. He just sees himself as being on an equal footing with her. Engaging with people person-to-person on a down-to-earth level—it's very important for him."[68]

LIFE IS MORE THAN YOUR JOB TITLE

Embracing a hobby like model train collecting illustrates another factor behind Wyss's lack of pretension: his commitment to living a full life outside of work. Wyss doesn't take himself too seriously, because unlike many leaders today, he has never allowed his role as a leader to define him. Regardless of the intense demands of the job at hand, he has always put clear boundaries around work and made time for a rich existence outside the company. When his daughter, Amy, was younger, he made a point of spending as much time with her as he could, even flying in monthly to visit her at college for the weekend. He also made time for his many hobbies other than model trains, including golf, skiing, tennis, art, travel, and of course, spending time in nature.

The passion he first realized in 1958 for hiking in the American West became especially important for Wyss as time went on, and would later come to occupy a good deal of his attention as a philanthropist. As part II describes in detail, when he was at his busiest—as CEO of Synthes during the mid to late 1980s—Wyss became connected with a group of friends dedicated to preserving wild spaces in Utah and elsewhere in the West. With these friends, he made regular one- to two-week expeditions into the wilderness, first in Utah and later in the Grand Canyon, enjoying the splendor he had first discovered upon coming to America.

Fellowship with like-minded people was a big part of the fun for him. Wyss would take his turn preparing a one-pot trail dinner, peering at recipes through reading glasses perched on the tip of his nose. Some of his hiking buddies still remember him charging up trails wearing his trademark red knee-high socks—a holdover from his youth in the Swiss Alps. "He loves being with friends and experiencing wilderness. I mean, he really just loves it," his former partner Marcey Olajos remembers. "The end of the day, no matter what we were doing, [would include] telling stories about the day with friends [over] a glass of wine or a little bit of scotch on the trail. He's a very easy person to be out there with."[69]

Beyond the chance to have fun with friends, Wyss cherished the experience of being out in nature, away from civilization, away from his office. As Wyss often says, he doesn't feel a spiritual connection with nature—he's not the type to experience existential revelations while climbing a mountain or seeing a beautiful sunset. But he does feel happy and refreshed when he's on the trail, and deeply appreciative of nature's beauty. "Art is everywhere," he says. "Some people see the wonderfully formed roots of a tree and consider it as art, and it is."

The rigors of hiking took Wyss away from his work, allowing him to see it with fresh eyes. Recounting a typical experience on the trail, he remarks, "It's so hot. My pack hurts—and here, this hurts. And then you say, 'Maybe I can't change it,' so maybe you start to think about a business problem." In fact, Wyss had some of his biggest intellectual breakthroughs while out in the wilderness. "It's the greatest way to make decisions," he says. "All the factors suddenly become very clear because you're not in an office, there is no phone, there is nothing."

The ideas he came back with were so good and plentiful that they sometimes left former Synthes COO Charlie Hedgepeth shaking his head in wonder. "I could sit at my desk all day long," Hedgepeth is reported to have said, "and not think of these ideas."

A QUIETER, SIMPLER APPROACH

Spending time in nature enabled an expansive sense of self that allowed Wyss to interact not just on a professional level with his people but on a *human* level. To those around him, he wasn't the "big boss"; he was a real person, sometimes maddening, but more often endearing and compelling.

Although their relationship was more formal during the early years, as time passed, Debbie Davis found Wyss to be a caring and supportive friend. During an especially difficult time in her life, Wyss called often to inquire how she was and to offer his help. "He's been very good helping me through it," she says. "He was just there for me, which was important to me. I mean, I couldn't have asked for anyone better, and I will always, always appreciate it."[70] Davis credits Wyss with expanding her life in many respects, including by teaching her "to really be very independent, which has been very important for me. He just has made me a very independent person."

In addition to his uncommon ability to connect deeply with others, Wyss's ability to see past his big title shows a striking lack of ego, softening his harsher side and making him more effective as a leader. When surgeons pointed out flaws in Synthes products or indicated their preference for a competitor's offering, Wyss didn't take it personally, react defensively, or try to convince the doctors they were wrong. Rather, he surprised them by inviting them to help him design a better product. Surgeons often accepted the invitation, resulting not merely in the formation of many new customer relationships but in the creation or improvement of many Synthes products.

As opinionated, decisive, and detail-oriented as Wyss is, he also was able to cede power to others in the organization without his ego getting in the way. "As a good leader," he observes, "you have to abandon power and give it to other people for certain decisions." A good example of this is the wide latitude he gave to Rick Gennett when he served as national sales manager. Recognizing Gennett's talent, Wyss let him coach the company's sales consultants and develop its sales strategies, intervening primarily when he felt that Gennett's budgeting requests were veering out of control. Wyss "always created loyal teams," Marcey Olajos says. "He understands what people are good at, and he gives them the room to explore paths to success. He likes empowering people."[71]

Wyss's lack of ego also came through in his determination to maintain a low profile for the company, and more recently for himself. He used to avoid drawing attention to Synthes within the industry, for fear of attracting competitors. Since his retirement, he has sought to avoid media attention for his philanthropic efforts, preferring to protect his and his team's privacy so everyone can focus on the work itself.

In recent years, as political adversaries have levied attacks, Wyss and the Wyss Foundation have been forced to pay more attention to their public image—a necessary measure to dispel the falsehoods that have circulated. The passing of time and the prospect of his own mortality have also changed Wyss's thinking about publicity, prompting him to attend more to his legacy and accept a more public role than he has previously. He still doesn't seek out attention, but when others honor him with recognition of some sort, he more readily accepts it.

"He's not looking to be a famous man at all," Rosamund Zander observed shortly before her death in September 2023. "He feels his power in getting things done."

In our publicity-saturated age, when so many people seek out fame while attempting to project images of power, status, and authority, Wyss reminds us that there's a quieter, simpler, and more honest approach to wielding influence and having a positive impact: Don't take what you do—or who you are—so seriously. Have fun and be yourself, quirks and all. Remember that you are more than your job title, your work, or your place in the organizational food chain. Infuse that broader, more fundamental sense of yourself as a human being into everything you do. See others as people on your level, and treat them with the compassion and respect they deserve. By leaning into your humanity, and by connecting with others on that basis as well, you'll wield more influence and have a greater impact than you ever thought possible.

5

HOW TO SAY NO TO $2 BILLION

Trust your friends (no matter how smart you are!) to expand your vision, identify blind spots, and keep you safe.

THE LATE 1980S AND 1990s were heady times for Synthes. Having solved many of its initial problems, including by building up a high-quality sales force and creating stateside manufacturing capacity, the company proceeded to take the US orthopedic surgery market by storm. Between 1987 and 1998, revenues for the company's AO-approved products ballooned from $64 million to $434 million, and the company expanded its product line to include implants for use in the spine and head (craniomaxillofacial).[72] In 1999, Synthes USA acquired Straumann's publicly traded medical business, Stratec Medical. The resulting entity, known as Synthes-Stratec, was a sizable public company traded on the SIX Swiss Exchange, with more than three thousand employees and annual sales of over 1 billion Swiss francs.

Such stratospheric growth piqued the interest of larger industry players. The global health-care giant Johnson & Johnson began to see Synthes-Stratec as a potentially attractive target for acquisition and initiated conversations with Hansjörg Wyss. By the early 2000s, Johnson & Johnson had offered Wyss $2 billion to buy the company.

At this point, Wyss owned Synthes-Stratec outright. During the late 1980s, he had paid over $50 million to buy out the company's other investors, and now he wondered: Should he take this opportunity to make a lucrative exit? Wyss wasn't sure. On some days he woke up interested in selling; on others he found himself dismissing the idea.

Christoph Megert, Wyss's personal attorney and friend, remembers discussing Johnson & Johnson's offer with him in Switzerland, during an hour-long drive from Bettlach to Basel. "Tell me, Chris," Wyss asked, "would you sell the company for that amount?"[73]

"You shouldn't ask me," Megert replied. "If someone offered *me* that kind of money, of course I'd say yes right away. But *you* shouldn't sell, because you dream of building a worldwide company. Until you've fulfilled that dream, you shouldn't think of selling."

Indeed, Wyss had long aspired to take Synthes USA global, which would entail acquiring Mathys, the other licensed distributor of AO Foundation products. His ambitions weren't primarily financial. In leading Synthes, he wanted to improve patient care by providing surgeons with the best possible internal fixation implants and tools and by supporting the AO Foundation's research and educational programs. And since the foundation depended on distributors for its annual budget, he recognized that any business threat to the distributors of its products also threatened the foundation and its good work. With competition fierce, Wyss believed that only a fully integrated global company would be able to sustain itself in the market over the long term.

The bottom line was this: If Wyss sold to Johnson & Johnson before acquiring Mathys, he would leave the AO Foundation vulnerable and jeopardize the core mission of both Synthes and the foundation.

While processing Megert's response, Wyss thought back to advice he received from his mentor and one of the AO's surgeon-founders, Martin Allgöwer. Allgöwer, too, recognized that for the AO Foundation to succeed with its mission into the far-off future, its distributors needed to be stable—and that this meant folding them into a single, global entity. Presenting a speech at a 1992 dinner, upon leaving his role as AO president and chairman of the board, Allgöwer had argued that the foundation's future needed to unfold along three core principles: "Bc magnanimous, speak the truth, and global Synthes."

Thanks to his conversations with Megert and others, Wyss wound up rebuffing Johnson & Johnson's offer. What really mattered was the AO Foundation and all that it worked for. A big payday would be nice, he reflected, but it could wait.

KNOW WHAT YOU DON'T KNOW

It's common today (in the tech industry especially) to mythologize successful business leaders as lone geniuses who make their mark by the sheer force of their personality and intellect.[74] Rather than acknowledge the efforts of an entire organization or culture, we like to attribute the magic of companies like Tesla, Apple, or Facebook to their charismatic founders. But as Wyss is quick to explain, the reality is much different. No matter how talented an entrepreneurial leader might be, they can't build a company alone or achieve any kind of sustained goal at scale.

"You need people around who support and help you," he says. "You also need people who protect you." Impact is a team sport, not an individual one.

Some might find it surprising—given Wyss's reputation as a strong, confident, and decisive leader who didn't hesitate to let others know when he felt that they were wrong—to hear him express vulnerability and extol the virtues of teamwork. "It's almost a paradox in that he was able to attract very skillful people within Synthes," says long-serving board member Bob Bland. "At the same time, everybody knew that Hansjörg called the shots."[75] But while he trusted his instincts, Wyss never relied exclusively on his own judgment. He is a deeply humble person who keenly senses the limits of his own thinking and understands the value that others can bring.

By the time he arrived at Synthes, Wyss had already made a practice of cultivating relationships with others who, by virtue of their age, subject-matter expertise, worldly experience, or intellectual sophistication, possessed insight that he lacked. Just as he fostered a critical, independent view of the world, he wanted to surround himself with smart people who felt confident in speaking their minds and critiquing *him* when necessary. "I didn't have any blind spots," he says, "and that's because I always had people around me who covered my blind spots."

While working one of his first jobs after graduating from Harvard Business School, Wyss had a boss who became addicted to drugs and was behaving erratically. To help him navigate this situation, Wyss turned to an attorney who was older than he was and who seemed to have the wisdom that he lacked. Similarly, during his early years at Synthes, he relied extensively on the counsel of Dr. Allgöwer. "I went to him, talked to him, at least two or three times a month," Wyss says.

Wyss also assembled a strong board composed of trusted confidants, and he turned as well to dedicated employees like Steve Schwartz (director of the Wyss Medical Foundation) and outside experts like Megert. Later, while launching his charitable foundations, he approached this new challenge in the same way: bringing in veteran operators in the conservation field as leaders and board members to help guide his giving, enabling it to have maximum impact.

SAYING NO TO "YES PEOPLE"

In Wyss's mind, a strong board of directors was an especially important source of wise counsel. "Even though I fully owned the company," he relates, "I was always very careful to have a board of directors, and further, to give them a lot of power. I presented all major investments to them. I presented all major plans to them and let them weigh in and let them have their say. And often, they helped persuade me that maybe that's not exactly the perfect plan. It's very important in leadership to let other people talk and give you advice and protect you from errors."

At many companies, board members might appear to be giving independent advice, but they really don't. Beholden to the board chair for their position, they often temper their remarks to affirm what they think the chair or investors want to hear. "That's not a good board," Wyss insists. "You need independent people who tell you what they really think." Wyss remembers specifically urging Synthes board members to regard his ideas critically and chastising them when he felt they were paying him too much deference. "If they pleased me too much, I said, 'You guys haven't thought this through. You're giving me too much freedom.'"

Wyss also was careful to run board meetings in ways that maximized contributions from others. "There was always the feeling among board members that Hansjörg would ask a question, and he would listen and sort of process that and make sure that he listened to the board members," former board member Felix Pardo says.[76] Former board member André Mueller agrees, saying, "Whether it was discussions where one could have different opinions or whatever, he made sure to hear everyone in the meeting before decisions were made." And as Mueller confirms, "There was no 'yes man' on the board."[77]

In addition to being independent, Wyss's board members gave him their best counsel because of the strong personal affection that had developed between him and them. "Nobody had a relationship in most companies like I had with my board members," Wyss says proudly. "They were like my brothers." In many cases, Wyss had worked with individuals for years or decades before appointing them to the board. When he brought in new board members from outside, he vetted them carefully to ensure that they would fit in well. He wanted advisors who would not just contribute to conversations but think independently—and challenge him when necessary.

As board member Bob Bland notes, Wyss has a special talent that allows him "to pick people who complement his skills but also that expand his vision."[78] Mueller, for example, joined the board in 2000 as a consequence of the acquisition of Stratec. He had little knowledge of the medical device industry, having spent his career in pharmaceuticals and biotech. He had never met Wyss before and was personally acquainted with only one other board member. Although Wyss had the contractual option of rejecting his candidacy, Mueller had a strong background in finance, and as Wyss apparently saw, he would be able to inject that expertise into discussions.[79] So, Wyss kept him on.

Over time, Wyss would get to know individual board members well by spending time with them outside of formal meetings: playing tennis together, inviting them to go skiing, having them to dinner. Even today, Bland and other former Synthes board members stay in touch with Wyss and think of him as a close friend. "He builds friendships, and he keeps them and maintains them," Megert says. "You could go have talks, have negotiations in the evening. We'd go to the kitchen and cook and have a glass of wine and tell stories. That's completely normal—respectful, always respectful, but very, very personal and very down-to-earth. He's fun to be with, but he is focused once you get onto the business side. He's focused and demanding."[80]

As board members recall, Wyss did more than the typical CEO and chairman does to make meetings fun, sociable, and memorable. In one instance, Wyss was convening the board in his hometown of Bern. At the beginning of the meeting's morning session, which took place in a hotel, he surprised everyone by asking, "Does everyone have swim trunks with them?" When some of the board members replied that they didn't, Wyss announced that the meeting would pause at noon, at which time those in need of trunks could run out and buy them. The meeting would then reconvene, running until about six that evening.

When six rolled around, board members walked down to the Aare River, which was well known to locals as a great place to bathe. The custom was to walk a bit up the river, jump in, and let the current carry you downstream. On this day, hundreds of people were enjoying the river. Since there were no locker rooms, the board members did as the locals did, leaving their clothes at river's edge to enjoy a friendly swim. The whole event was a treat, something unusual and unexpected for most of the Synthes board members. "I've had a number of occasions where he surprised the people, the board, with his initiatives," Mueller says. "And that also creates a lot of empathy and teambuilding."[81]

Wyss values independent counsel so much that he willingly—indeed, enthusiastically—assented to oversight from an additional body: a technical commission composed of AO/ASIF doctors. Synthes USA's agreement with AO specified that before the company could sell any new products, AO had to formally approve it through this commission. Another CEO might have chafed at this restriction, but Wyss loved it. He could be sure that the world's best surgeons had thoroughly vetted every new Synthes product and suggested any necessary improvements—*before* it went out to market.

At first, the commission's AO doctors were unpaid, which lent a sense of purity to their deliberations. Eventually Wyss did pay royalties to some of these doctors, a choice that reflected the depth of their contributions as well as his fear of losing them to competitors. Yet even in these cases, he already knew the doctors involved, and felt certain that they would only approve products that truly improved the standard of care patients received. The technical commission "was a real strength," Wyss says, offering exceptional quality control. Because of its oversight, Synthes never had to recall a single product during his tenure.

A MATTER OF TRUST

Although Wyss valued the opinions of board members and other confidants, he never felt beholden to them. When he disagreed with counsel that he had received, he went his own way. Often his judgment proved correct, but sometimes it didn't.

Once, Wyss proposed to the board that the company start a new line of spine-related products and sell them through a large existing sales force that was dedicated to Synthes maxillofacial products. Using the existing personnel would save the company from having to invest millions in establishing a new sales force. The board advised against this move, arguing that these consultants were already accountable for a specific line of products and that it would be disruptive to assign them a new and very different line. Wyss respectfully disagreed. At the time, the company had only one spine-related product, so he thought they could get away without a special sales force dedicated to it.

With the board's consent, Wyss executed his plan. Within eighteen months, it was clear that the board had been correct: The maxillofacial sales force wasn't succeeding with the spine-related product. Sales consultants weren't interested in cultivating spine surgeons as clients because they earned their commissions through strong relationships they'd already established with regular orthopedic surgeons. Wyss went back to the board and acknowledged that his plan wasn't working. He and the other board members considered whether to do what the board had originally counseled: invest in establishing a new, dedicated sales force for the spine business.

A pivotal moment in the discussions came when Steve Schwartz, who was responsible for overseeing sales of the spine-related products, reported on what he'd seen during a recent trip to California. Working with members of the sales team had convinced him that Wyss's plan would never succeed. But when Wyss asked him to share his opinion with the board, Schwartz tried to put a good face on the progress the sales teams had made.

"No, no, no," Wyss said. "What do you *think*?"[82]

Realizing that Wyss wanted his honest, unvarnished advice, Schwartz didn't hesitate: "I think the current model is effed up, and we need to create a separate sales force for spine."

"OK, go do it," Wyss replied, assenting to the more costly plan that his board had originally supported. Schwartz executed the plan, and in short order the spine business was growing rapidly.

"These decisions look easy, but they're very difficult," Wyss reflects. "You need a group of people by your side to give you guidance—[people] who review a business issue objectively, without any personal stake in the decision or axes to grind. And you in turn must place your trust in them."

HOW A DEAL GETS DONE

One of the most difficult decisions Wyss faced during his time leading Synthes arose during the late 2000s, when he again found himself pondering whether to sell the company. The situation was different this time—and more favorable to selling.

On the one hand, Wyss had achieved many of his long-term goals for the company. In 2004, he had completed the acquisition of Mathys, finally succeeding in unifying the AO Foundation's distributors and making Synthes a global company. And in 2006, he had secured AO's future—and positioned Synthes as a more attractive acquisition target—by engineering a deal to acquire patents for the products it sold. AO had long held those patents, in addition to the Synthes brand name, but the price was right: a one-time payment of $1 billion to the AO Foundation. Now, instead of relying on annual royalties paid by Synthes to keep the lights on, the AO Foundation could fund its annual budget by drawing on earnings from a massive endowment. Synthes would also provide smaller annual payments in exchange for the foundation's continued provision of educational instruction.

Selling also seemed like an attractive option because market conditions had shifted, creating new challenges for the company. Laws in key European, Japanese, and US markets had changed, making it harder to get regulatory approval for new medical devices. Facing pressure from insurers, hospitals were becoming more cost-conscious and less willing to pay for updated (and more costly) products when older ones would do.

Wyss enjoyed running the company, and he had shepherded it through many years of strong growth. By 2010, Synthes sales had risen to almost $4 billion, and the company employed over eleven thousand people in the United States and dozens of countries around the world.[83] But Wyss wondered if these new conditions would make it more difficult for Synthes to achieve the same kind of success going forward. Having reached his midseventies, he had run the company for almost forty years. Perhaps it was a good time for him to sell and pass the baton to another company and its leaders.

During the fall of 2010, company representatives, overseen by long-serving board member and Wyss confidant Amin Khoury, began shopping the company to interested parties, including direct competitors, larger health-care manufacturers, and private equity firms. Meanwhile, Wyss began a months-long process of personal deliberation. He had devoted the bulk of his career to building this company, creating billions of dollars in value. Was he really ready to give up control over it? Was his analysis of the business climate accurate, and if so, was selling a better option than trying to grow by acquiring other firms? And what would he do with himself when he no longer had a global company to run?

To process these questions and come to the best possible decision, Wyss turned again to board members, trusted friends, family members, and other confidants. "I talked to everyone I could," he says. "It's a difficult decision. You can't make it emotionally; you have to do it rationally." Wyss knew that his board would stand behind whatever he decided—he had long ago demonstrated his unique ability to size up business opportunities and exercise sound judgment. As he talked through the opportunity with board members, he found that they all agreed with his hypothesis: Selling now was probably the right move. They did push him to think about the emotional dimensions of selling and whether he was ready—useful questions that, in Wyss's words, "helped me figure out whether I really wanted to sell."

As time passed, Wyss became convinced that selling was the right move. Meanwhile, the sales process narrowed down to two potential buyers: Johnson & Johnson and a consortium of private equity firms. Johnson & Johnson seemed to be the better option due to its financial position and familiarity with Synthes's business, but Wyss wanted to be sure to get the best possible price. Here again, he relied on his circle of close confidants, talking through each step of the negotiation process with them.

In addition, rather than negotiate with Johnson & Johnson himself, he nudged them to deal instead with Khoury and other company representatives, by having members of his board spread the word that he could be extraordinarily emotional and difficult to deal with. Although this was true, it was also a highly strategic move: Staying in the background while his trusted colleagues negotiated the deal would leave open the opportunity for him to play the "bad guy" and push back should parts of Johnson & Johnson's offer prove problematic.

In the end, this approach worked. In April 2011, the companies announced that Johnson & Johnson had agreed to acquire Synthes for $21.3 billion. When the deal closed the following year, it was worth slightly less: $19.7 billion, still almost $4 billion more than what the private equity firms had offered and nearly *ten times* the $2 billion price floated by Johnson & Johnson a decade earlier.[84] Once again, Wyss had made shrewd business moves that would enable him to create value and ensure that the company's mission would live on long into the future. And once again, he had done it with the help of others.

It's great to be a strong, independent thinker, but all of us have blind spots, gaps in our knowledge, and limits to our wisdom. To make fewer mistakes and maximize our impact, we need others around us to scrutinize our thinking and offer frank feedback. No matter where we are in our career, we can all keep an eye out for others who might serve us well as advisors, mentors, or confidants. The time and energy required to form true and lasting friendships is an important investment in our future effectiveness as advocates and change-makers. If we learn to value wise counsel now, building up a network of advisors, we'll have trusted, long-term friends whom we'll be able to count on years or even decades from now, when we really need them.

PART II

SAVING NATURE FOR ALL

6

WHERE LOVING A PLACE WILL LEAD YOU

Drive progress by making sure the public benefits (not just a privileged few) and empowering ordinary people to fight for what is theirs.

ASK HANSJÖRG WYSS ABOUT his favorite outdoor experiences, and he'll regale you with accounts of hikes through Arizona's Grand Canyon, in particular along the technically demanding Royal Arch Loop. It's a place so exquisite that the National Park Service describes the trail as being "replete with more natural beauty than humans can absorb," while also offering "about a million ways to get into serious trouble in a remote part of the Grand Canyon."[85] Picture breathtaking desert vistas, sheer red-faced cliffs lined with vegetation, massive boulders, and small basins formed of gently undulating sandstone ridges.[86] Apart from other hikers you might happen to meet, there's no sign of human civilization as far as the eye can see. It has looked this way for a thousand generations.

The arch is "the most interesting approach into the Grand Canyon," Wyss asserts. In his telling, you hike through an oak forest and eventually come to the top of a red wall, which stands hundreds of feet above the river below. You're looking for a way down, and you see a hole with a tree rising up inside it. This is a trail that the ancestral Puebloans, an ancient Indigenous people who settled in the area, used to access the river.

"You climb into this hole, and you're in the dark basically," Wyss says. Holding on to the walls and the tree, you "inch your way down" about 150 feet, "and if you let go, of course, you're dead. But we were all very skilled." At the bottom, you find yourself on the top of a steep slope comprising dirt and loose rock. You descend farther to the riverbed, climbing over boulders, and continue until you reach the first watering hole, where you pitch your tent and spend the night.

Wyss isn't content to regard wilderness from a distance, out of the window of a passing car or from the cockpit of a plane. He wants to lace his boots over his red knee-high hiking socks and experience nature viscerally. "He's just really fun to hike with," says Jamie Williams, president of The Wilderness Society. "He doesn't want anyone making a fuss over him. He is steady on. He can out-hike anybody. He just loves it."[87] Even the most rugged of terrain doesn't intimidate him. A lifelong athlete who grew up hiking in the Alps, he has the climbing chops, physical stamina, and calm demeanor to see him through challenges that novices might regard as terrifying. "You go out with Hansjörg, and you're probably in for a real expedition," remarks Bill Hedden, former executive director of the Grand Canyon Trust. "He connects to the place by loving the place."[88]

For Wyss, loving a natural place doesn't mean having a meditative, reflective, prayerful experience. Rather, it's about reveling in beauty, much as one might enjoy a favorite work of art. Trips to the Grand Canyon have also always been social experiences for Wyss. In terrain like this, it would be dangerous to travel alone, even for an experienced hiker. You need others around to watch your back and help out if you run into trouble.

Marcey Olajos remembers how, toward the end of one Grand Canyon expedition with Wyss during the late 1980s, the group encountered a "very treacherous" part of the route, with "no trail, a lot of climbing, and loose rock." The sun was going down, and members of the group were worried—it was still a long way back to the parking area. Wyss "just calmly took control of the situation," Olajos says, recalling the cold, the darkness, and how nervous they were. "We ended up hiking with flashlights. And he is a great orienteer. He can figure out where he is at any given point in time. He's just got a sense for that. And he got us back there."[89]

Just as important, experiencing wilderness in the company of good friends adds to the fun. Wyss recounts how, in the Grand Canyon, a long day of hiking always culminated in a relaxing cocktail hour. "Everybody brought an appetizer for the group. Everybody made sure they had a little bottle of whiskey."

TURNING AFFECTION INTO ACTION

The Grand Canyon is part of the Colorado Plateau region of the United States, straddling portions of Colorado, Utah, Arizona, and New Mexico. Wyss first encountered portions of this region in Colorado during his initial visit to the United States in 1958. During the 1980s, as he was working to build Synthes into a fast-growing medical device company, he became involved with the Southern Utah Wilderness Alliance—which has defended Utah's historic desert wildlands from oil and gas exploration and other threats since 1983—and hiked throughout southern Utah with people he met through the organization. By the late 1980s, he had joined the board of another regional conservation group, the Grand Canyon Trust, which has worked since 1985 to protect both the land and the rights of the area's Native peoples, and had begun exploring the Grand Canyon with his hiking buddies.

One of the Grand Canyon Trust board members was John Leshy, former general solicitor for the US Department of the Interior. He traces Wyss's global conservation efforts in recent decades back to his love for this region and its breathtaking, unspoiled natural landscapes. The sheer size of these landscapes evidently made quite an impression on Wyss. As he told *National Geographic* in 2019, "You just can't believe, when you come from a country that is only 2,400 square miles, and you see these places, and you see the sky changing. It's just unbelievable."[90] Leshy surmises that the Colorado Plateau also attracted Wyss because unlike in Switzerland, "there are large swaths of no obvious signs of human habitation—no mining, no logging, no hydroelectric dams, et cetera—I think that really appealed to him."[91]

Another aspect of the Colorado Plateau also attracted Wyss, so much so that it would profoundly shape his future philanthropy: These were vast *public* lands, protected by the federal government to remain open and accessible to all. Wyss believes strongly that enjoyment of nature shouldn't be just for wealthy private landowners—it should be for everyone. As President Theodore Roosevelt put it at the turn of the twentieth century, after establishing several national parks that helped lay the groundwork for America's National Park System, "Our people should see to it that they are preserved for their children and their children's children forever, with their majestic beauty all unmarred."[92]

Thinking back to his childhood, Wyss recalls that he and his family were able to enjoy nature wherever they wished because Swiss law dating from medieval times allowed all citizens to access natural lands even when they were privately owned. Although some restrictions on hunting were in place, anyone could walk through private forests or fields to forage for mushrooms, collect fallen branches for use as firewood, or simply enjoy a bit of serenity. In the United States, by contrast, property rights are more stringent and exclusive, giving rise to the familiar No Trespassing signs. Fortunately, huge portions of land are still publicly owned and managed. Anyone who wishes can enter them and enjoy their wild, unspoiled beauty.

Wyss's hiking trips in the Colorado Plateau during the 1980s and early 1990s left him with a strong desire to protect the public lands he treasured and to *keep* them wild for future generations. Then as now, the pristine character of this land was under threat, whether from recreational vehicles or from the desire of commercial interests to use the land for mining, grazing, or fossil fuel extraction. Meanwhile, suburbs were expanding into private lands that had formerly been fields or woods, leaving millions of people without easy access to nature. Wyss felt it his duty as a human being to conserve these places for others to enjoy. And thanks to the success of Synthes, he now had the means to support groups fighting to manage public land properly and conserve it as wilderness.

"Somebody needs to do it," he says when asked about his core motivation as a conservationist. "Simple as that. Somebody needs to conserve beautiful places. There are a lot of NGOs [nongovernmental organizations] that do it and work on it. There are not enough individuals who are rich who do it. So, I decided that this is what I want to do."

During the early 1990s, Wyss began making donations of about $5,000 to $10,000 to local and regional groups dedicated to protecting public lands in the Colorado Plateau. The first check he wrote, Wyss recalls, was a $5,000 gift to The Wilderness Society. Six months after he made the donation, one of the organization's leaders called and asked to visit him in Pennsylvania to solicit future gifts. Wyss turned down the offer. "Are you actually going to waste money on a train or flight from Washington, DC, to Pennsylvania?" he asked. "Why don't we just continue talking on the phone, and you can ask me for what you want."

The leader made the request, and Wyss agreed to make a larger donation the following year. But he advised—somewhat arrogantly, he now thinks—that executives at the group forgo travel and fundraise over the phone instead. Even then, Wyss wasn't interested only in giving away his money but also in making sure that these important organizations were making the best possible use of it.

In addition to providing financial support, Wyss became an active and engaged board member not merely at the Grand Canyon Trust but also at The Wilderness Society and the Southern Utah Wilderness Alliance. "I don't think Hansjörg ever missed a board meeting," says Ed Norton, founding president and board member of the Grand Canyon Trust. "He was very, very, very conscientious about being a board member and being on the board, and being very much engaged in what the organization was doing."[93]

Wyss was especially interested in applying his business expertise to help these groups operate more efficiently and effectively. He noticed, for instance, that these organizations tended to adjust their staffing up or down on a short-term basis, depending on how many donations they received during a given year. This constant fluctuation was highly disruptive. Not only were these organizations constantly dealing with staff turnover; being always on the defensive, reacting to financial pressures, left them unable to think and behave strategically. Wyss solved this problem by convincing the organizations to manage their money better, putting portions of the donations they received into a reserve fund that would grow and allow them to cover annual fluctuations in income. The change gave each group new stability, and rather than spending their time hiring and firing people and worrying about short-term budgets, the leaders were free to work on strategy.

MOBILIZING GRASSROOTS SUPPORT

Wyss's support for public lands took an important turn during the mid-1990s, thanks to changes in Washington, DC. In 1993, President Bill Clinton tapped former Arizona governor Bruce Babbitt to become his new secretary of the interior. In this role, Babbitt bore responsibility for agencies such as the National Park Service and the Bureau of Land Management (BLM), which oversees hundreds of millions of acres of federal land. A devoted conservationist, Babbitt perceived that congressional deadlock would prevent the passage of any big environmental legislation for the foreseeable future. But he was pleasantly surprised to learn that the administration might be able to use existing laws, most notably the Antiquities Act, in new ways to protect large tracts of wilderness.[94]

Signed into law by President Roosevelt in 1906, the Antiquities Act provided the first legal framework in the United States for protecting cultural and natural resources on federal lands. Roosevelt used the act thirty-six times to establish national monuments, including Grand Canyon National Park; he was the first of eighteen US presidents, including both Democrats and Republicans, to protect public lands in this way.[95] Babbitt had the idea to use the Antiquities Act to designate tracts of land currently managed by the BLM as national monuments, to be set aside for conservation purposes under the BLM's protection. Existing infrastructure could remain on these lands, as well as previous activities such as grazing or hunting, but nothing new could be undertaken—no new mining, drilling, road building, or real estate development. The wild character of these places would be preserved.

Although the BLM was already responsible for sensitive wilderness areas, it was known not for conservation but for allowing commercial activities such as mining, grazing, and logging. Babbitt, however, envisioned the creation of a new system of protected lands within the BLM whose presence in turn would transform the agency into a new force for conservation. The country needed to protect entire landscapes, he felt, not just parks, and as steward over the largest amount of federal land, the BLM was the agency to do it.

Babbitt felt that working with the BLM might also foster grassroots support for conservation initiatives, because the agency had a stronger record than other federal agencies of working with local communities and allowing multiple uses on its land. Although environmentalists had little love for the BLM, Babbitt believed the agency held potential. "The BLM is an agency full of a lot of different kinds of people," he said, "and many of them would be happy to perform to higher standards. What they need is some leadership and an opportunity and some incentive."[96]

Influenced by Babbitt, President Clinton in 1996 turned to the Antiquities Act to create the Grand Staircase–Escalante National Monument. Located in southern Utah and encompassing 1.7 million acres of BLM-managed wilderness, the monument was the largest ever created in the continental United States. The announcement of the monument's creation, conceived with Clinton's upcoming reelection campaign firmly in mind, won plaudits nationally but fell flat with many Utah residents. The administration had done little advance work at the local level to explain the monument and its impact, or to gain the support of local groups. Many residents bristled at the notion that the federal government could just come in and unilaterally change the status of lands that they and their communities relied on economically. Utah senator Orrin Hatch condemned the administration's action as "the mother of all land grabs" undertaken "without so much as a by-your-leave to the people of Utah."[97] Even local environmentalists were upset at the lack of consultation. "All kinds of people I work with are angry about the process that didn't happen," one said.[98]

In the wake of this controversy, environmentalist and conservation groups knew they needed to build support for future monuments that the Clinton administration was planning to create across the American West. Local group members rose to the challenge, attending public meetings, writing op-ed pieces in community newspapers, persuading their public officials, and so on. Wyss helped to fund these efforts, supporting an array of groups on the ground that were supporting conservation and monument creation in western states. The broader point wasn't simply to give everyone access to land but also to give ordinary citizens a hand in securing it—to affirm democratic principles by tapping popular, grassroots sentiment in favor of conservation efforts.

Eager to build on that success and create even greater impact, Wyss created the Wyss Foundation in 1998 to formalize and deepen his giving, bringing in a former official from Babbitt's Department of the Interior, Geoff Webb, to run the organization. The foundation's mission, as articulated in internal documents from the early 2000s, was "to preserve, protect, and restore the public lands, waters, and open spaces of the American West to achieve ecological health across the landscape and build community, maintain diversity, and nourish the human spirit."[99] With that mission in mind, the foundation made grants during its early years to local groups such as the New Mexico Wilderness Alliance (now known as New Mexico Wild), the Nevada Wilderness Project, and the Montana Wilderness Association (now known as Wild Montana), funding the work these organizations were doing to build support for new monuments in their communities and to hold the BLM accountable for managing existing ones responsibly.[100] After all, it was one thing to create monuments but quite another to implement the intended land protections. Local activists would need to remain vigilant and focused, and Wyss's ongoing support would help to ensure that they were.

Molly McUsic, who was counselor to Secretary Babbitt, told the story years later (at a Wyss tribute dinner) about the profound difference the Wyss Foundation made on the ground in those early days. After proposing a national monument in Arizona, known as the Grand Canyon–Parashant, McUsic and the interior secretary traveled to Flagstaff to meet with local citizens about the proposal, expecting that former governor Babbitt would be received with pride and fanfare. They were wrong. By the end of the meeting, local residents "were practically insulting Secretary Babbitt's mother," McUsic recalled. "We were so finished."

But the Wyss Foundation was not deterred. "Hansjörg and his team were just getting started," McUsic says. "They commissioned a poll that showed overwhelming support for a monument in Arizona. They got it picked up in *The Arizona Republic*; it triggered a wave of good stories. Positive editorials followed. Citizens lobbied the delegation. Supportive crowds appeared at meetings. The delegation's opposition softened. We made the monument. People loved it. . . . I really want Americans to know what they owe to that man."[101]

SOLIDIFYING A NEW PUBLIC LANDS SYSTEM

Buttressed by Wyss's funding of grassroots efforts, the Clinton administration would go on to create or expand twenty-two national monuments using the Antiquities Act, setting aside six million acres of federal land for protection.[102] Further, in 2000, Babbitt created via secretarial order the National Landscape Conservation System (NLCS) to administer these new national monument lands and prioritize them for conservation. By combining the lands into one system, the administration would raise its public profile and increase the odds that Congress would provide the funds necessary to manage them well.[103]

Yet creation of this system was hardly a permanent solution. Because it was brought into being by secretarial order, any future secretary of the interior who might be less friendly to conservation could come along and abolish the NLCS, leaving the lands protected by the Clinton administration vulnerable to development and exploitation. And when the Bush administration took over in early 2001, it appeared that this scenario would play out.

Like his father before him, former Texas governor George W. Bush had ties to the oil industry. So did his vice president, Richard "Dick" Cheney, who had served as the CEO of Halliburton, a giant in the oil field business. The Bush administration was notably friendly toward corporate energy and mining interests. Based on their early public statements, federal officials seemed eager to reverse the massive conservation gains made during the Clinton era, rolling back specific monuments and undoing the NLCS.[104] Although some administration officials later denied interest in rescinding the monuments' status, the Bush administration did seem poised to shrink the size of individual monuments or to allow mining and other activities that the Clinton administration had prohibited on these lands.[105]

Faced with the specter of new energy extraction projects marring pristine wilderness, the conservation movement in the West was on the defensive. Wyss and his friends were determined to push hard to preserve the gains spearheaded by the previous administration.

To ensure that lands already protected under the Antiquities Act saw no new development, the Wyss Foundation continued with its democratic, boots-on-the-ground approach, funding dozens of watchdog organizations at the local level to advocate for conservation. "It was a real grassroots effort to stop all the rollbacks" of monuments, says Chris Killingsworth, executive vice president of the Wyss Foundation. "Supporting the local groups to come together and make their voices heard was critical."[106]

As Ed Norton explains, the Wyss Foundation's basic premise was that "places with special attributes—natural wildlife, cultural, [and] historic places—regardless of their statutory designation are best protected if there is a local organization that is their advocate."[107] Local activists know and care about the individual places at issue. Their presence in their communities puts them in a strong position to advocate for greater protections while also pushing back against commercial interests seeking to develop local lands.

To lead its efforts in support of local groups, the foundation brought Killingsworth and McUsic onto its staff. Both individuals were well respected in the conservationist community and had played key roles in the creation of the new monuments. All told, by 2002, through its support to local conservation groups, the Wyss Foundation had helped to create virtually all the monuments established during the Clinton era. Staff members had an intimate understanding of the lands and of the complex legal and bureaucratic issues involved in protecting them. If anyone was equipped to fight back against the potential rollbacks, it was the Wyss Foundation.

The foundation began to increase the funding available for local groups, which formerly had been scattered. "You go and find people who are already doing this work," Killingsworth says. "They're just doing it with no money, up against an oil company. No money. No organizing. No legal help. Nothing. And so you find them, and you help resource them."[108] In 2007, the Wyss Foundation brought local conservation groups together into a national network, helping to launch and funding the National

Conservation System Foundation (later renamed the Conservation Lands Foundation) with a board that included prominent conservationists such as Ed Norton, Bruce Babbitt, and former US secretary of the interior Stewart Udall. With the Conservation Lands Foundation's support, every major portion of the lands overseen by the BLM now had a local "friends of" group aggressively advocating for conservation and against development. These groups also mobilized to support the NLCS.

Unfortunately, conservationists' fears about the George W. Bush administration's threat to roll back protections on public land did come to pass. As one observer wrote in 2003, "The Bush administration's management of public lands thus far includes greater resource extraction, greater accommodation of development interests, and fewer environmental protections." Among the administration's moves during its first two years alone was proposing a plan to allow logging in the Giant Sequoia National Monument, which includes more than five hundred square miles of some of the most ancient, majestic trees on Earth; loosening restrictions on ecologically destructive mining practices on public land; and preventing any new lands in the American West from being considered as protected areas.[109]

President Bush did end up signing certain bills that kept public lands safe from development and established new national monuments that protected large portions of US territorial waters.[110] Still, all told, Bush's two terms in office saw nothing less than "an assault on public lands," as one commentator put it, including a dramatic increase in the amount of BLM land leased to energy companies for fossil fuel extraction.[111] And with each attempted rollback of conservation measures, local groups supported by the Wyss Foundation and other funders stepped up to fight back.

Later, when the Obama administration came to power, the advocacy of these groups led Congress to pass the Omnibus Public Land Management Act of 2009, which codified the National Landscape Conservation System and thereby ensured that future presidential administrations couldn't easily unwind it. The act also added two million new acres of land to be conserved, so now the BLM had to manage these lands for conservation purposes. Bruce Babbitt's original vision, strongly supported by Hansjörg Wyss, was finally in place.

Since then, the Wyss Foundation has continued to fund the Conservation Lands Foundation, which in turn has helped to ensure proper management of these lands and to add millions more acres to the system. In reflecting on the dominant leadership role played by Wyss, McUsic likes to quote Abraham Lincoln: "He who molds public sentiment, goes deeper than he who enacts statutes or pronounces decisions. He makes statutes and decisions possible or impossible to be executed."[112]

Despite the setbacks of the Bush years (as well as President Donald Trump's later attempts to undo public land conservation), recent decades have seen a marked increase in the amount of protected public lands in the United States: from about 350 million acres in 2000 to 400 million in 2020.[113] In considering this record, it's hard to overstate the impact of Wyss's efforts to conserve land managed by the BLM. Had it not been for the Wyss Foundation's funding of advocacy, many of these lands would now be much more highly developed. There would be mining, road building, and off-road vehicles encroaching on vital animal habitats. Southern Utah, for instance, would look radically different. "When we did the Grand Staircase National Monument in 1996," John Leshy says, "it was the most remote place in the lower forty-eight states—the place furthest from a paved road. It's still that way. And it wouldn't be if not for Wyss's efforts."[114]

McUsic echoes these sentiments. As she observed in her 2011 tribute to Wyss, "This is more than increasing the number of acres under protection. These lands have their own distinct mission; they preserve the past. They will not be tamed for tourists. No lodges, no gift shops, no fast-food restaurants. There are mule deer, elk, and bears, and hunting, and grazing, cowboys on horseback. If you're on these lands, you're in the Wild West. . . . It still is the way it was. And it wouldn't have been that way if it hadn't been for Hansjörg."[115]

Wyss has also made the conservation movement healthier, funding dozens of thriving conservation groups across the American West, both individually and through the Conservation Lands Foundation (which today supports more than eighty advocacy groups in the western United States). As Leshy points out, Wyss's philanthropy also has helped to transform the BLM into a "big conservation agency," with tens of millions of acres now managed primarily for conservation and wilderness protection.

Wyss's efforts to safeguard public lands hold lessons for changemakers everywhere: Regardless of where we enter the conversation, whatever our cause or concern, we can maximize impact by focusing on questions of access and by ensuring that the benefits we're providing or advocating for accrue to the broadest possible constituency. Often, we need not create a whole new resource to make a difference, but rather can protect those that our governments are already holding in the public trust. And instead of trying to exert influence from above, we can work from the ground up—by collaborating with and empowering ordinary people in local communities to become more engaged and active. We can make small donations or volunteer our time with local groups fighting to protect public spaces, improve public health, revitalize public education, and more.

Hansjörg Wyss fell in love with the Colorado Plateau. And when you love something, you can't help but want to share it with everyone else and enlist as many like-minded people as possible to protect it.

7

A CROWNING ACCOMPLISHMENT

Refuse to think small! Pursue change at the greatest possible scale available to you.

DURING THE 1830S, A trapper named Osborne Russell ventured into southwestern Montana and found "a smooth valley surrounded by a high range of mountains" that was populated by "many buffalo." Since time immemorial, Indigenous tribes such as the Blackfeet, the Bannock, and the Crow had used this valley as their hunting grounds, leaving behind tepee rings and other artifacts as evidence of their presence.[116] A generation or so after Russell, a few other adventurous souls came to the area to raise cattle, founding some of Montana's first ranches. One of these ranchers, a woman by the name of Rachel Orr, was so moved by America's one hundredth anniversary and the centennial celebrations that in 1876 she called the area the Centennial Valley. The name stuck. By the turn of the century, homesteaders had arrived and established the town of Lakeview, which at its height counted nearly four hundred residents.[117]

Today, the Centennial Valley still looks much as it did back then.[118] Ten to twenty ranches remain, accounting for over one hundred thousand acres, and the federal government owns most of the land, including the forty-five-thousand-acre Red Rock Lakes National Wildlife Refuge. The valley is a haven for many species, including moose, swans, wolves, and grizzly bears, serving as a vital geographical linkage for animals migrating from the Yellowstone National Park area over into parts of Idaho.[119] But at a time of rampant suburbanization across the American West, there's a reason why the Centennial Valley remains largely untouched: because a community of local people has cared enough about this landscape to want to save it. And that's because one man—Hansjörg Wyss—decided to dream big and support an innovative approach to protecting wild spaces.

During the early to mid-2000s, the Centennial Valley's large, family-owned ranches faced economic pressures to sell off portions of their land to developers.[120] These ranchers care deeply about the natural character of their lands, and they weren't eager to see the valley become mauled by the construction of large resorts and vacation homes. They wanted to hunt and fish on their lands and use it for grazing, just as generations of their families had done before them. Still, the ranchers had bills to pay, and real estate values were high.

The Nature Conservancy began to work with individual ranchers, exploring whether it might be feasible to compensate them in exchange for conservation easements, agreements between a private landowner and a land trust that protect in perpetuity a property's land, wildlife, and ecology. In other words, an easement allows a property owner to maintain ownership and control of the land, while designating how it will be used and protected, for both today and tomorrow. To make easements work, the organization would have to find outside donors to pay for the easements. And that's where Hansjörg Wyss came in.

In 2006, after meetings between Jamie Williams (then director of The Nature Conservancy's programs in Montana) and representatives of the Wyss Foundation, a ranch owner had been found who was ready to agree to a conservation easement. Other big donors might have just written a check, but Wyss wanted to visit the land first and understand the project in detail. The project's novelty made delving into the specifics especially important. The Wyss Foundation had been supporting local conservation groups for nearly a decade by then. During the early 2000s, it had begun to acquire land for conservation as well, making small purchases in Oregon and Montana to be transferred to government entities. But the foundation hadn't yet funded easements as a conservation tool. Some board members were hesitant. Each conservation easement agreement was different, and unless the contract was properly written, it might not sufficiently protect the land.[121]

In August 2006, Wyss and other foundation members traveled to the Centennial Valley to discuss the project.[122] A rancher graciously hosted the group in rustic cabins that were nestled on her land, at the end of a dirt road amid breathtakingly beautiful grasslands. As John Leshy remembers, the scenery was spectacular, a "very impressive place."[123] Meeting with Williams and his team, Wyss asked thoughtful questions about the deal, but he also wanted to know about The Nature Conservancy's plan for the whole valley. Wyss wasn't interested in saving just one parcel of land, as satisfying as that might be. To maximize his impact, he sought to invest in ways that would save an entire landscape.

Unrolling a map, Williams detailed for Wyss how The Nature Conservancy hoped to engage both private and public money to secure a series of contiguous conservation easements on the portions of the valley that were privately owned. Williams discussed the terms of the easements, noting that if all went according to a community-driven plan, the entire landscape could be well protected over a period of several years. Wyss inquired how much funding the project would require from him, both for this first easement and for the others to follow, should The Nature Conservancy manage to secure them. Williams told him, and Wyss agreed to commit the full amount toward the project: $6.5 million.

At Wyss's insistence, Williams arranged for him to meet with local ranchers who were working together on a shared conservation vision for the valley and approved of the easements. "He really likes hearing from local folks," Williams says. "He appreciates learning about their vision, and understanding the depth and breadth of the partnerships that exist there." At the meeting, Wyss listened deeply, saying little beyond offering a few words of support and encouragement. He was honored to be in the presence of locals who were working hard to conserve this wondrous place, and as Williams remembers, his deep respect came across "in a very genuine and warm way."[124]

Over the next few years, many of the local ranchers signed up for easements, collectively protecting tens of thousands of acres of land. One large ranch didn't participate, but fortunately that parcel of land was being well managed and today remains ecologically intact. The Nature Conservancy was able to secure government funding through the Land and Water Conservation Fund (LWCF)—established by Congress in 1964—to match the money that Wyss donated. The partners also worked with local ranchers and the US Fish and Wildlife Service to create an easement acquisition zone in the valley, which facilitated the project. Thanks to these efforts, the Centennial Valley today remains unspoiled by developers. Ranchers can enjoy their traditional way of life, and the integrity of the landscape will remain intact for generations to come.

THE LARGEST PRIVATE LAND DEAL IN US HISTORY

It's easy for philanthropists or activists to follow familiar roads that require little innovation but don't necessarily yield the most progress. But as Wyss understands, we have much to gain by aiming for change at the greatest possible scale available to us. Wyss welcomes big, seemingly insurmountable challenges, relishing the opportunity to figure out new solutions at scale. Former Synthes employee Eric Lohrer observes that Wyss the engineer and entrepreneur "just enjoys trying to make things happen. He likes to see something through that only he, with his wealth and his approach, can make successful."[125] Wyss's thinking is simple: Why should we satisfy ourselves with incremental improvements when we could be doing so much more? Indeed, don't we have a *responsibility* to do as much good as we possibly can with the resources at our disposal?

Although initially the Wyss Foundation's goals were small, focused primarily on the Colorado Plateau and on protecting the new national monuments, Wyss expanded the foundation's efforts during the 2000s to include land protection across the entire western United States. The idea was to save big landscapes using whichever tactics and strategies would prove most durable and effective.

At the time, nobody else in philanthropy was focused on protecting land at scale, so it seemed worthwhile and important to fill the gap. Besides expanding public enjoyment of land to the greatest number of people, preserving large tracts of land for public use would be an effective way of addressing a range of other pressing issues such as climate change, environmental degradation, and the biodiversity crisis. Although implementing industrial regulations that restrict emissions, penalize polluters, foster green energy, and the like is crucial, simply saving large tracts of land makes a massive—and sometimes underappreciated—difference. It does so in a number of ways, including by storing carbon in the land, preventing the emission of carbon that would come from development, and protecting wildlife and their habitats.[126]

The Centennial Valley wasn't the only area where the Wyss Foundation attempted large-scale conservation during the 2000s. Farther north, Wyss spotted an opportunity to safeguard the Swan Valley, a landscape within the vast Crown of the Continent ecosystem. The Crown's importance is hard to overstate: It comprises the single-largest intact ecosystem in the continental United States, still providing refuge for every plant and animal species that Lewis and Clark encountered during their historic initial exploration of this land in the early nineteenth century.[127] The ecosystem stretches from Montana north into British Columbia, straddling the Rocky Mountains and encompassing both protected and unprotected lands. Toward the east is the Rocky Mountain Front, whose prairie lands are prime habitat for grizzly bears. Along the western portion is mountainous terrain, and in the southwestern corner is the eighty-mile-long Swan Valley, with its lush forest surrounded on both sides by steep, white-capped mountains.

During the early 2000s, the Swan Valley area was under siege. A big landowner in the area was the Plum Creek Timber Company, which owned 640-acre plots of land interspersed with plots of government-owned land in a checkerboard pattern. During the nineteenth century, the federal government had granted these squares of land to railroad companies, hoping to incent them to build tracks across the country. The railroads in turn sometimes sold off these lands to timber companies and other players. Now the Plum Creek Timber Company was planning to sell off portions of land it had acquired in the Swan Valley, for the creation of small ranchettes. Before long, vacation homes and hotels would dot the valley floor where wildlife had long roamed. Local residents feared that the valley's rural character would fundamentally and permanently change, impacting wildlife and also their own ability to use the land recreationally.

To prevent this outcome, a conservation group called the Trust for Public Land (TPL) began buying up small plots of land at market prices as Plum Creek Timber put them up for sale. But too much land was coming up for sale too quickly. "We couldn't keep up with the pace of protection," said one resident and local activist. "How in the world were we ever going to muster the political and financial wherewithal to figure out a big-scale solution?"[128]

TPL approached the Wyss Foundation, seeking funding for these purchases. Reviewing past deals, Wyss and other foundation leaders realized that TPL was paying retail prices for these lands, which made them extremely expensive. Unless the organization could negotiate lower prices, it wouldn't be economically feasible to acquire all of Plum Creek Timber's land in the Swan Valley for conservation.

Eager to figure out a solution, Wyss Foundation representative Chris Killingsworth met with Jamie Williams and connected his organization, The Nature Conservancy, with TPL. The Nature Conservancy was a bigger, better-financed organization than TPL, and Killingsworth thought that if the two worked together, they might be able to help devise and execute a more comprehensive plan. The groups also joined forces with The Wilderness Society, a national leader in public land conservation, and community groups who had been leading local collaborative conservation efforts for decades.

In 2006, the groups convened a meeting of philanthropists—including the Wyss Foundation—to share their initial thinking about how to save bigger chunks of the Swan Valley and to solicit help. The foundation responded positively, but along with other funders it challenged the groups to devise a plan that would somehow save the *entire* valley. One local resident present at the meeting remembered their message as follows: "Either protect the whole Swan Valley or we're not interested."[129]

Over the next few years, the groups rose to the challenge, devising an arrangement that became known as the Montana Legacy Project. The groups identified lands both inside the valley and beyond that were owned by Plum Creek Timber and that were the most important ecologically and to the community. By June 2008, Plum Creek Timber had agreed on terms to sell 310,000 acres of its land at cheaper, wholesale prices. The groups then held dozens of community meetings to get input on who should own these lands and how they should manage them. As a result of this collaborative, trust-building process, the groups agreed that the land would ultimately go into state and federal management and that Plum Creek Timber would still be able to harvest trees for a period of years.

To arrange for funding, the groups approached government officials, receiving a warm reception from Governor Brian Schweitzer and US

Senator Max Baucus. These leaders and others in Montana were deeply concerned that without this ambitious plan, the piecemeal sale of Plum Creek Timber lands would close off land that had been formerly open to the local community for hiking, fishing, and hunting. "It was going to change the face of western Montana if this model kept rolling on," Jamie Williams remembers. This was "an all-hands-on-deck moment."[130]

Baucus and Schweitzer arranged for federal and state support, but the deal would only go through with additional monies from philanthropic funders. Thus it was that Hansjörg Wyss flew in to meet with Williams and state officials, who tried to convince him to participate. After all, this would be a historic undertaking: the largest private land deal in American history.

Wyss and others from the foundation remember arriving at Holland Lake Lodge, a small, rustic lakeside resort with unforgettable views of two mountain ranges, which advertises that when it first opened in 1924, it was "a two-day stagecoach ride from Missoula."[131] Wyss hadn't been told exactly why he'd been asked to come, but he was assured that if he waited a bit, all would become clear. At around two in the afternoon, a helicopter landed, and Governor Schweitzer stepped out. Then another arrived, bearing Senator Baucus's staff.

"Why are you here?" Wyss asked.

"Well," they said, "we want you to protect the whole Swan Valley."

"How big of a project is it?"

"Probably about $500 million."

"I really can't spend $500 million on the Swan Valley."

"Well," they said, "that's why we're here."

Governor Schweitzer and Senator Baucus said they could secure at least $350 million in federal and state funding. They needed $100 million more from private donors. After touring the valley that afternoon and enjoying a nice dinner, Wyss agreed to give $25 million of that remaining $100 million, and if they couldn't find other donors, he'd consider adding more. Further, he'd arrange for a prominent friend of his to perform due diligence on the deal, to ensure that they weren't paying too high a price to the timber company.

"This was a worthy project," Wyss says now. "If Montana puts up money and Baucus puts up money, why shouldn't I do so?"

Acquisition of the lands took place in stages, with the first portion of the deal closing in March 2009. In the end, Wyss donated $35 million and was the largest private funder. His contribution was pivotal, unlocking enough funding from other philanthropists to allow the deal to proceed. As Jamie Williams reflects, Hansjörg Wyss's funding "made the impossible possible. It gave us the confidence to solve a problem that the local communities and conservation community didn't know how to solve on their own. And then he stuck in there with us to close the deal."[132] Without Wyss's energetic support, some land might well have been conserved—but it certainly wouldn't have been the largest private land deal the United States had ever seen.

SAVING MORE WITH A MOVE NEVER SEEN BEFORE

As important as the Swan Valley project was, it turned out to be just the first in a series of initiatives that conserved land in various portions of the Crown of the Continent. Like the Swan Valley deal, each of these projects was massive in scale, protecting tens or hundreds of thousands of acres of environmentally sensitive land. These projects continued to stretch the Wyss Foundation, mobilizing an array of conservation tactics—some quite novel—to get the job done.

While some of its peers put heavy restrictions on the tools they were willing to use, the foundation prided itself on pursuing its goals by using *all* tools at its disposal, including ones that may have been unfamiliar at first. It was important, Wyss felt, to flex to the circumstances, using tools that might be necessary in specific situations even if they were unhelpful elsewhere.

During the late 2000s, for example, the Wyss Foundation saw opportunities to buy oil and gas leases to protect land in the Badger-Two Medicine area of the Rocky Mountain Front, a region located on the eastern side of the Crown of the Continent. Many of these leases, which dated to the Reagan era, had generated fierce resistance from the Blackfeet Nation, a nearby Indigenous people, and conservation groups. Because of this opposition, drilling never took place in these areas, and in 2006 the government suspended future leasing.[133] Yet the drilling rights remained intact, which meant that the land in question might still be drilled at some future time. To prevent this from happening, the Wyss Foundation helped conservationist groups negotiate buyouts of leases and, in some cases, for oil companies to donate their rights. Between 2007 and 2023, all the existing oil and gas leases in the Rocky Mountain Front were permanently retired, protecting roughly 160,000 acres.

During the early 2010s, the foundation also helped to protect 10,000 acres along the Rocky Mountain Front that were in the hands of private ranchers, by working to arrange for and fund conservation easements. David Carr, a longtime employee of The Nature Conservancy in Montana, conducted painstaking work on the ground to identify sensitive lands, build relationships with the ranchers who owned them, and come to easement terms that met their needs while also conserving the wilderness. He credits the Wyss Foundation for funding the purchase of easements and for supporting conservation groups that were trying to secure more federal funding for easements through the government's Land and Water Conservation Fund.[134]

At the same time, the Wyss Foundation was working hard to protect other areas of the Crown. In 2011, the foundation agreed to buy out oil and gas leases in portions of the Flathead River area, protecting a total of 300,000 acres. In 2015, the foundation helped The Nature Conservancy purchase more than 117,000 acres in Montana's Lower Blackfoot River watershed. The deal, part of the conservancy's Great Western

Checkerboards Project, also allowed for the acquisition of almost 50,000 acres in Washington State.[135] Remarking on the diversity of approaches the foundation used to protect areas of the Crown and elsewhere, Killingsworth notes, "We trained ourselves, sometimes bringing in people to help us learn. Hansjörg gave us the freedom to try a bunch of different approaches and see what works."[136]

As of today, nearly 440,000 acres of privately held land in the Crown of the Continent have been protected with the Wyss Foundation's help. Combined with national parks and other protected public lands, the amount of protected wilderness exceeds four million acres. David Carr estimates that, all told, conservation efforts have affected about 70 percent of the landscape around the Crown. And even that is just the beginning. Over the past decade, the foundation has applied what it learned in the Crown to save pristine landscapes elsewhere in the western United States—and (as the next chapter reveals) around the world.

Reflecting on conservation in the Crown, Carr regards it as "easily the greatest conservation story in modern times in the lower forty-eight, and probably globally significant. You've got this fairly highly intact landscape that's been protected and that wouldn't have been had we not had the Wyss Foundation's help. And in most cases, it was all done working with communities and getting their buy-in."[137]

Jamie Williams regards Wyss's contribution to the American West and the Crown in particular as a singular legacy of conservation. "I think he really took conservation to scale," Williams says. "He arguably could be seen as having the biggest impact on the protection of wild landscapes in the American West of any single person, certainly during my lifetime."[138]

Project	Description	Acres Protected
Rocky Mountain Front and Badger-Two Medicine oil and gas lease buyouts, donations, and lease retirements, 2007–2023	Ensure that areas of the Rocky Mountain Front and Badger-Two Medicine will not be exploited for fossil fuel extraction.	160,000
Montana Legacy Project, 2009–2010	Protect the entire environmentally sensitive Swan Valley of Montana and other area lands.	312,000
Hoback Valley, Wyoming, 2012	Partner with the Trust for Public Land to protect big-game habitat via oil and gas lease buyouts.	Almost 50,000
Yurok Blue Creek Salmon Sanctuary, 2013–2017	Purchase land to create a salmon sanctuary for the Yurok Tribe.	25,000
Great Western Checkerboards Acquisition, 2015	Help The Nature Conservancy purchase unspoiled forests and rivers in Montana's Blackfoot River watershed.	117,000
Sabinoso Wilderness, 2015, 2019	Purchase two properties abutting the Sabinoso Wilderness area in New Mexico. These properties doubled the size of the wilderness area and allowed it to be open to the public for the first time.	13,100

Select Wyss Foundation conservation projects in the United States, 1998–2023

MOBILIZING OUR PARTNERS

There's another, less obvious way that Wyss has impacted conservation in the American West and beyond: through the Land and Water Conservation Fund, which funds the acquisition of public protected lands and supports outdoor parks and recreation projects at the state and municipal levels. As the Department of the Interior puts it, the fund serves to "strengthen communities, preserve history, and protect the national endowment of lands and waters."[139] The 1965 legislation that created it authorized the Department of the Treasury, for a period of fifty years, to earmark for the LWCF up to $900 million of federal revenues annually from federal properties and from offshore oil and gas drilling. States and municipalities could in turn obtain grants from the LWCF to build or sustain local parks or to protect local lands large and small.

During the first decade of the LWCF's existence, Congress earmarked significant sums each year for it, but funding languished during the decades that followed. Throughout the 1980s and 1990s, combined annual funding for land acquisition and state grants hovered around $300 million or less, representing only one-third of what the legislation had originally envisioned. Although funding briefly spiked at the turn of the twenty-first century, it declined again during the 2000s.[140] As a group of individuals and groups that support the LWCF noted in 2019, Congress siphoned off over $22 billion in funds over the fund's lifetime that was intended for the acquisition and protection of wild spaces, using it for other, unrelated purposes. This in turn "means that our public lands, waters, and historic sites have missed out on billions of dollars—putting places we love in peril."[141]

During the late 2010s, as Wyss began putting together big land conservation deals, he spotted an opportunity to unlock large amounts of federal money for future deals by drawing attention to the LWCF. Although philanthropies such as his were doing good work at scale, the availability of hundreds of millions of dollars more in federal funding each year would prove a boon to conservation efforts across the United States, complementing philanthropic money and helping to make more big deals possible. "Private money can only do so much," says Andy French, conservation program officer at the Wyss Foundation. "Having that program fully funded, with mandatory funding, would be a big deal. Synching up federal support with philanthropic foundations—that's how you can get a real impact, bolstering groups' acquisition work in the United States."[142]

Most Americans knew little about the LWCF and its importance in safeguarding wild places. If Wyss could draw public attention to the fund via an educational campaign, grassroots pressure might build, inducing policymakers to take two key steps: one, make the fund permanent, and two, make it mandatory for Congress to earmark the full $900 million each year.

By 2010, the Wyss Foundation was funding some conservation groups to help conduct public education campaigns in support of the LWCF. With the fund set to expire in 2015, the foundation intensified its support for public education campaigns, which ultimately helped groups to secure a three-year extension for the fund. In 2017, with the extension now set to expire, the foundation galvanized others in the conservation community to rally support for the LWCF. These efforts again bore fruit. On March 12, 2019, the John D. Dingell Jr. Conservation, Management, and Recreation Act—named for legendary Michigan congressman and conservation champion John Dingell, the longest-serving member of Congress in American history, who had died a month earlier—authorized the LWCF permanently.

At this point, the Wyss Foundation had a choice to make. It had achieved its first goal for the LWCF, but it still hadn't secured the mandatory $900 million annual appropriation. Should the foundation be satisfied with this victory and pause its funding? Or should it keep fighting for that full $900 million, knowing that with both the Oval Office and the House and Senate majorities held by Republicans—a party that historically has sided with development interests over conservation—this effort would be an uphill climb?

The foundation opted to continue funding public education related to the LWCF. "Everyone kind of constantly laughed us out of the room, saying, 'This will never happen,'" French recalls.[143] Nevertheless, the foundation persisted, funding groups whose public education and advocacy campaigns kept a constant drumbeat of attention focused on the LWCF. Two groups in particular—The Nature Conservancy and the Open Space Institute—were paramount in organizing other, smaller groups to mobilize on behalf of the LWCF. Their education campaigns included tactics like making sure that publicity around local land conservation deals included mentions of the LWCF, so the public would understand and appreciate the fund's importance. The groups also created a national map that allowed people to appreciate the full scope and scale of LWCF-funded projects.

In 2020, the Wyss-funded groups' work around the LWCF finally paid off when the Great American Outdoors Act was signed into law, fully funding the LWCF. For the first time in its history, the LWCF was fully funded *and* permanent, a feat that, in the words of The Wilderness Society president Jamie Williams, represented "an unprecedented opportunity and obligation to use the Land and Water Conservation Fund to make meaningful progress" on a variety of economic, equity-related, and environmental goals "while protecting our most treasured places."[144]

To date, this victory has bolstered conservation efforts across the United States, in part by increasing conservation projects in the pipeline. Landowners who might be thinking of selling their lands for conservation purposes now have assurance that sufficient federal funding is in place to complete the deal, so they are more inclined to pursue that path. The assurance of funding also means that acquisition projects funded by the Wyss Foundation and others can now protect more acres and proceed more smoothly and quickly to completion.

As Wyss's experiences with both the Land and Water Conservation Fund and the Crown of the Continent teach us, it helps to have money or other resources at our disposal when trying to make change, but money is not nearly enough. Even more important is a willingness to harbor grand ambitions—and a stubborn determination to see them realized. We must be willing to take risks in service to these ambitions, operating in areas where others aren't inclined to go. Further, we must be willing to adjust our tactics and even to learn entirely new ones. And we must do everything in our power to bring partners to the table who can magnify our impact. In our digital, globalized world, it's easier than ever to effect change at scale, even when we don't have billions of dollars at our disposal. But we'll never achieve such lofty goals unless we set aside our ingrained assumptions about what is possible and *dream big.*

The scope of change can't be our only consideration. Other factors also shape the kind of progress we can achieve. Informed by its experiences saving the Crown, the Wyss Foundation today deploys a multipronged "conservation blueprint" when evaluating potential projects. The first criterion concerns the size of the potential impact: The land being protected must be a significant landscape—large, wild, and intact—that safeguards carbon stocks. But the foundation also considers a slew of other factors when choosing what to fund, including whether the projects offer enduring protections, whether they are feasible in a reasonable time frame, and whether they safeguard (or if possible, expand) the sovereignty and rights of Indigenous people and local communities consistent with the conservation goals. Such factors—beyond just a question of projected size—help to shape a project's ultimate impact on the world.

Let's challenge ourselves to analyze critically the opportunities available to us, forgoing easy, established ways of making a difference that don't really enable that much change. When opportunities arise to unleash true transformations, let's act on them quickly, even if they seem a little risky. In particular, let's strive to engage in areas where others aren't focused, serving needs that might be going unfulfilled. And let's become more engaged in the details of our philanthropic or activist projects, as this will increase the likelihood that they'll eventually deliver the big results we envision.

Most of us can't hope to save an area as vast or as important as the Crown of the Continent. But if we push ourselves to think and act big, and if we mobilize others to work alongside us, we can achieve crowning accomplishments that make the most of our talents and the resources available to us.

8

HOW A RANCH WAS SAVED AND YOUNG CONSERVATIONISTS WERE MADE

Focus not just on your own actions but on how to generate long-term impact by empowering rising generations of activists.

OREGON'S PRISTINE JOHN DAY River, billed by the Bureau of Land Management as "one of the longest free-flowing rivers in the continental United States,"[145] is a haven for rafting enthusiasts, who will enjoy floating along its trail for decades to come. Entering at Cottonwood Canyon State Park, they'll wend their way downriver through exquisite canyons and grasslands that provide sanctuary to bighorn sheep, deer, hawks, and other animals.[146] They'll hop out at a point known as the McDonald's Ferry river access, effectively the last place they can easily exit. From here, the river flows for ten miles through terrain bereft of roads and parking areas. It eventually runs through dangerous Class VI rapids before reaching Tumwater Falls, which is too high for boats to pass.

Future rafters might not realize it, but their ability to have fun and immerse themselves in nature on this portion of the river owes to the efforts of an energetic young conservationist named Alex Barton. Growing up in a small, rural town in New Hampshire, Barton enjoyed being outdoors but grew concerned at seeing parking garages and large commercial buildings being built on land that had previously been forest or wetlands. After graduating from Bates College with a degree in environmental studies and anthropology, he decided to pursue a career conserving wild spaces. He helped build trails in Arizona, New Hampshire, and Montana and then went back to school, earning a master's degree in natural resources and conservation from the University of Montana. From there, he got his first professional job in the conservation field, coming on board as an associate project manager at the Western Rivers Conservancy (WRC), a nonprofit that purchases lands along rivers in the western United States and then secures money to transfer them over to state and federal agencies or Tribal Nations for permanent conservation and recreational access.[147]

As a recent graduate, Barton served the organization as an all-around utility player, performing due diligence on deals and identifying sizable parcels along the John Day River that would be suitable for conservation. Once he found such parcels, he cold-called the landowners to see if they might be interested in selling their land to Western Rivers Conservancy. One of those whom Barton contacted during his second year on the job owned a parcel on the John Day River, called the McDonald's Ferry Ranch.

The property's name derives from a ferry that operated during the nineteenth century, helping some of the four hundred thousand pioneers traveling on the historic Oregon Trail—in the largest mass migration of people in American history—to cross the river. The current landowner lived a few hours away and had been using the ranch as a private getaway, but now he was interested in conserving the land. Over a three-year period, Barton helped to negotiate a deal to acquire, thanks to funding by the Wyss Foundation, the 4,100-acre property and arrange for its subsequent conveyance to the Bureau of Land Management (BLM).

As Barton explains, the deal's closing in the late summer of 2023 represented a significant gain for local conservation efforts.[148] The previous owner had graciously allowed boaters to move through his land, traversing from the river to a nearby road, but subsequent private owners might not have been so generous. By acquiring the property, Western Rivers Conservancy and the BLM ensured that future generations of boaters could continue to access the river between Cottonwood Canyon State Park, a previous WRC project, and the McDonald's Ferry Ranch. Safeguarding this property also opened it up for hikers, fishers, hunters, and other outdoor enthusiasts, especially important given the relative lack of public land in the area. Furthermore, because of the ranch's location, protecting it would also allow the BLM to restore a once productive steelhead tributary. The project complemented WRC's previous acquisitions on the John Day that collectively protected nearly thirty thousand acres of shrub-steppe habitat, over thirty miles of river, and dramatically expanded recreational access to the lower John Day.[149]

The McDonald's Ferry Ranch deal was the first conservation deal Barton had helped to complete and, as such, was a considerable point of pride for him. Many twentysomethings go into public service dreaming of one day making a meaningful difference, but Barton had actually done it. "One thing I love about the work I do is that it's extremely tangible," Barton says. "This ranch is a property that we shifted from private to public land and now becomes open to the public. It's safeguarded from potential adverse development. It's habitat for wild animals, and it's available for future restoration. I just love that."[150]

There's someone else who played a role in the conservation of this slice of the John Day River: Hansjörg Wyss. Were it not for him, Alex Barton might not have ever come to work at Western Rivers Conservancy. As it turns out, Wyss played an important role in supporting Barton's career at two critical junctures: when he was a graduate student at the University of Montana, and a bit later, when he had graduated and was seeking his first job. As a student, Barton earned a spot in the Wyss Scholars Program, a scholarship offered by the Wyss Foundation and administered by universities that pays for half of the student's tuition and expenses. Students can apply if they attend one of six universities with a strong reputation in the conservation community. Master's students receive half of their award while they're still in school and the other half if they become employed in the land management or conservation field.[151]

Becoming a Wyss Scholar was pivotal for Barton. From his initial experiences, he knew it would be hard to break into a professional career in conservation without a graduate degree. When he entered the University of Montana, he had little savings, and the program didn't offer any funding to help students with tuition or living expenses. By deciding to enroll anyway, Barton took a chance on himself, trusting that he would somehow figure out a way to pay for his education. As he is quick to acknowledge today, if he hadn't been named a Wyss Scholar, he would have emerged from graduate school with a crushing amount of debt. But thanks to the Wyss Scholars Program, rather than going to work in a more lucrative field to pay off his loans, he was free to pursue his dream of saving natural spaces.

Once Barton graduated and began looking for a job, he again crossed paths with the Wyss Foundation. As he discovered, Western Rivers Conservancy was hiring for a two-year position that was 80 percent funded by the foundation as part of its Wyss Fellows Program. The program is designed to help train early career professionals in the conservation field by partnering them with a host organization and an experienced mentor at that organization. It also provides Fellows with periods of training to help them build skills in communications and advocacy as their career advances. Conservation groups apply to the Wyss Foundation to host a Fellow, who must work on conservation issues somewhere in the United States. Once the foundation grants a group's request, the group hires for the position just as it would for any other job. The Fellowship lasts for two years, after which the hosting organization may choose to bring the Fellow on staff permanently at its own expense.

For Barton, starting as a Wyss Scholar and then becoming a Wyss Fellow opened up a pathway into a rewarding career in the conservation field. His two years in the Wyss Fellows Program immersed him in the details of land acquisition and conservation project management and allowed him to make valuable contacts in the field. Happily, once his Fellowship ended, Western Rivers Conservancy was able to hire him for a permanent position as a full-time field representative.

A couple of years after that, Barton was promoted to project manager and made responsible for developing his own land acquisition deals. He also took on a government relations role, helping the organization's president build relationships with congressional staffers and officials at federal agencies. The Wyss Fellows Program was "enormously impactful," Barton says, given how difficult the job market in the conservation field was at the time for recent graduates. He was able to establish himself in his desired career and, in relatively short order, to make a tangible difference as a conservationist.

INVESTING IN CONSERVATION'S FUTURE

During the mid-2000s, while Hansjörg Wyss was helping to protect hundreds of thousands of acres of wilderness in the western United States, he also was thinking more broadly about the future of the conservation field. To constrain those who wanted to develop wildlands, it wasn't enough for a few wealthy philanthropists to protect specific plots. As Wyss saw it, the country needed a thriving conservation movement that could galvanize local communities to care about nature. That in turn meant encouraging future generations of smart, ambitious young people to choose a career in conservation and to take on a leadership role.

It can be difficult for young people interested in conservation to pursue careers. Specialized graduate degrees have become much more expensive, and many of the best programs have little financial aid available. Students exiting these programs often do so with barely manageable amounts of debt, which sometimes forces them to sacrifice their dreams and take better-paying jobs outside the conservation field. Once young people graduate, opportunities to break into the conservation field can be scarce. Many local organizations are small and running on tight budgets. They need new hires to jump in and make important contributions immediately. They can't afford to give young professionals time to learn the basics of the job from established practitioners. When young people look at job listings, they often find that entry-level roles require two to three years of experience, presenting them with a dilemma: How can they get that experience if they can't get a job in the first place?

In 2005, the Wyss Foundation began to address these problems by creating the Wyss Scholars Program. Initially, the program worked with two participating schools with strong conservation degree programs: the University of Montana and Yale University. In 2007, the foundation expanded the program to include the University of Michigan and Northern Arizona University. A decade later, it would expand again to include two law schools specializing in conservation, the University of Colorado and Lewis and Clark Law School in Portland, Oregon.

In 2008, the foundation took another bold step, creating the Wyss Fellows Program as a way of bringing energetic and passionate young talent into the conservation community—both recent graduates and individuals who had experience in other fields but were looking to shift into conservation. Serving as a Wyss Fellow, a young person would gain those valuable first years of experience that might make them attractive to organizations hiring at the entry level. In choosing organizations to host Fellows, the Wyss Foundation paid special attention not only to the good work the group was doing but also to whether it had someone in place who could offer helpful guidance and support to the Fellow. Heath Nero, senior program officer at the Wyss Foundation and a former Wyss Scholar at the University of Michigan, notes that the idea behind the Fellow program was to "give new people a positive experience so that they'll want to stay in conservation, with someone overseeing them who is excited and a good mentor."[152]

Over the years, the scope of these programs has expanded with that of the Wyss Foundation itself. From its initial work to conserve public lands in the Intermountain Region of the United States, the foundation had expanded its efforts by the late 2000s to include conservation efforts throughout the country. (And during the 2010s, as the next chapter reveals, it would extend its reach yet again, supporting conservation efforts around the world.) Similarly, the Scholars and Fellows programs evolved to support conservation across the United States, not just the West (these programs are still limited to the United States as of this writing). Organizations seeking to host Wyss Fellows also now operate in areas across the country.

MAKING A DIFFERENCE

These two programs have only existed for the better part of two decades, but their impact on the conservation field has been significant. As of 2023, 193 individuals have been named as Wyss Scholars, while eighty have become Wyss Fellows. The vast majority of the Scholars have been able to find initial jobs in the field and receive the second portion of their award payment. As for the Fellows, 81 percent of them continued work in conservation after completing their Fellowship, for either a nonprofit group or a government agency, while 5 percent got involved in private-sector conservation work. "Those are pretty good numbers," says Kellie Shanaghan, conservation program associate at the Wyss Foundation. They show that "the program is effective at bringing in new people to work in conservation—and at keeping them there."[153]

The impact goes well beyond the numbers. Alumni of these programs describe the tremendous effect the awards have had on their lives and careers. The ability to graduate with less debt gives them the freedom to pursue conservation work that they are passionate about, without worrying as much about the pay or how to get a start on their financial lives. Alumni report that the ability to network with other Wyss Scholars and Fellows expands their understanding of conservation while also supporting their personal growth and career opportunities. Others describe how these programs boost their self-confidence, helping them to think of themselves as budding conservation leaders.

The late Julia Elkin, who worked with the Marin County, California, Department of Public Works as a sea level rise planner, remarked, shortly before her passing in early 2024, that receiving a Wyss Scholar award was the "defining moment" in her career: "It encouraged me to see myself not just as a hard worker with a passion for the environment, but as a conservationist with leadership capacity. That mindset shift guided my decision to go into public service, where for the past seven years I've supported and led climate change adaptation projects along the California coast."[154] To honor Elkin, an endowment in her name has been established at the University of Michigan, with support from both the university and the Wyss Foundation. The endowment will help to support graduate students financially during their internships so that they can gain on-the-job training in the conservation field.

For Grecia Nunez, serving as a Wyss Fellow while still in her midtwenties was an opportunity to sharpen her career goals as an advocate for underrepresented people impacted by environmental issues. At New Mexico Wild, Nunez worked as a community organizer in southern New Mexico, building support among local community members for measures to protect the Gila River—the last major free-flowing river in the American Southwest—and the many rare animal species that use its habitats. Her experiences taught her how important it can be for activists to come into local communities and build strong, respectful relations with residents, listening to their views, understanding their concerns, and jointly thinking through the impact of conservation measures.

Building on her Fellowship experiences, Nunez is now pursuing a law degree at American University in Washington, DC, with the goal of working in climate change law. "I'm really interested in the displacement of people due to climate change," she says. "There are no legal protections for these people. If I have a dream job, it's working for a nonprofit doing policy work around that."[155]

The Wyss Fellows Program has also helped the conservation community by strengthening local organizations. Founded in 2017, the Oregon Desert Land Trust acquires and conserves private lands in the southeastern portion of the state, known as the "high desert region." With fewer than ten staff members, the trust operates as a start-up, and staff members such as executive director Brent Fenty juggle multiple roles. Fenty describes how the arrival of Wyss Fellow Kharli Rose as outreach coordinator made a big difference in the organization, boosting its impact well beyond expectations for its modest size. Thanks to her previous career in local news broadcasting, Rose was prepared to help build the Oregon Desert Land Trust's communications program from the ground up, including understanding the organization's target audiences, developing its brand and messaging, writing its regular newsletters, and helping develop its long-term communications strategy.

In applying to host a Wyss Fellow, Fenty had hoped to identify someone he could hire permanently after the Fellowship period ended, and in Rose, he found that person. For a small organization like this, the financial support to bring in a key hire and establish that person in the organization was important. "It's rare that you find a commitment like this for two years that covers 80 percent of a [job] position. That gives us the ability to really launch this new position. We have two solid years of having someone onboard and teaching them the skills, and then being able to convert that to a full-time position. It's outstanding."[156]

Anecdotally at least, the Scholars and Fellows programs seem to be contributing significantly to the conservation field's talent pipeline. One former Wyss Scholar, Patrick Holmes, served on the staff of former Montana governor Steve Bullock as a natural resources policy advisor. Other Scholars and Fellows have worked for conservation groups both large and small as well as for government agencies like the US Forest Service and the National Park Service.[157] These young leaders aren't just clocking in; like Alex Barton at the Western Rivers Conservancy, they're making tangible contributions. "If you look at the Fellows and Scholars who have come through our program," says Nero, the Wyss Foundation senior program officer, "they're some of the most effective people in the conservation community."[158]

Greg Zimmerman, a former Wyss Scholar at Yale and now the director of the Protection Campaign at the Resources Legacy Fund, observes, "If you look out across the conservation community, certainly that part of it that's working on public lands—it's filled with people who were either Wyss Scholars or Fellows."[159] After working with several former Wyss Fellows, Zimmerman understands how vital mentorship and a chance to build relationships inside an organization can be to the career of a budding conservationist, just like for young professionals in every field. If these programs cease to exist, he notes, "the pipeline of professionals who are committed to doing this work will slowly begin to dry up, and maybe that pipeline won't be replaced."

Thankfully, these programs do exist, and that's thanks to the wisdom and generosity of Hansjörg Wyss. As astonishing as it is to say out loud that Wyss is directly responsible for the conservation of one hundred million acres, in fact that's quite a conservative estimate—it only takes into account his direct impact. Looking at what he has done for the conservation field generally, we see that his true impact is far greater.

As Wyss understands, it's one thing to advocate for change using the resources at your disposal. But we can do so much more by inspiring and empowering other like-minded people to mobilize their energies and talents as well. And by investing in young people, we can activate change well into the future. Wyss has done this not only in conservation but in other areas that are important to him: At Synthes, he supported young, high-potential surgeons who were doing pioneering work on patients' behalf. In his personal philanthropy and in his business affairs, he has helped young people realize their dreams by funding scholarships and offering career opportunities. Because he also cares deeply about the arts, as chapter 12 describes, he has funded scholarships for budding musicians at the Boston Philharmonic Youth Orchestra and funded a school for the visual arts in Switzerland.

Although we may lack the financial means to fund educational opportunities in areas that matter to us, all of us can help build the next generation of change-makers in other ways. All of us can volunteer to teach a course at our local high school or community college or to serve as a mentor in our community. Or we can create summer job or internship opportunities at our company, or invite children into our organization for a day to discuss important issues and the work our colleagues are doing. Anyone can agree to sit for an informational interview when a young person requests it, or reach out to kids in our daily life, asking about their interests and encouraging them to follow their dreams. These kinds of actions take time, and they don't yield results immediately. But they do bear fruit.

Any progress we manage to make isn't worth very much if we can't sustain it. And one powerful way of sustaining it is by creating more pathways for young people to make exciting contributions of their own.

9

THE MAGIC NUMBER IS THIRTY

Seek to achieve not just the improbable but the impossible—
which may be more possible than you think.

THERE ARE BIG CONSERVATION efforts, and then there are *really* big ones—such as the most significant initiative ever undertaken to save our land, water, diversity of species, and open spaces. This agreement, under which nearly two hundred countries pledge to protect 30 percent of all land and oceans on planet Earth by 2030, is known as 30x30. It came about at the 2022 United Nations Biodiversity Conference, thanks to years of patient effort on the part of environmental groups, policymakers, and local communities across the world. But some might be surprised to discover that it wouldn't have happened without the ambition, generosity, and vision of Hansjörg Wyss.

The story of 30x30 begins during the mid-2010s, following Wyss's successful 2012 sale of Synthes to Johnson & Johnson. He had stepped down from the CEO role five years earlier but had remained chairman of the board, so the deal now represented an important inflection point in Wyss's life, leaving him both much wealthier and fully retired. He was in his mid-seventies, still vigorous and healthy. With no business to occupy his mind, what would he do next? Others in his position might have decided to relax and enjoy a well-earned retirement, with perhaps a handful of donations to worthy philanthropies and regular community volunteer efforts to pass the time. Wyss had a different agenda. Having immersed himself in conservation causes through his foundation, he now saw an opportunity to become more personally engaged as a philanthropist and to have an impact that was bigger and broader than anything he had achieved thus far.

During the 2010s, Wyss would venture into whole new areas of philanthropy, making grants to groups pursuing a range of social justice causes and expanding his giving in medicine, academic science, women's health, and the arts (as described in part III of this book). But he also ramped up his efforts in the conservation space, developing projects beyond the United States that preserved large tracts of land for public use. In 2014, the Wyss Foundation began what would become a long-term commitment to improving the management of African wildlife parks, supporting ten parks in seven African countries by pledging more than $160 million in grants to the African Parks Network. In 2015, the foundation began another long-term commitment to permanently safeguard wilderness in the Amazon region of South America, helping to launch what would become known as the Andes Amazon Fund; nine years later, the project had permanently protected more than thirty-six million acres of pristine land in Ecuador, Columbia, Peru, and Columbia.

As important as these philanthropic efforts were, Wyss found that he wasn't satisfied. It was one thing to advance conservation in a local area or region, even a large one like the Crown of the Continent. But given the resources that he now commanded, Wyss aspired to push himself harder and deliver impact on an even greater scale. And what greater scale than a threat to the very planet we live on?

By the mid-2000s, countless scientists were issuing dire warnings about the existential threat posed by a looming global biodiversity crisis. Plant and animal species were now estimated to be disappearing at a rate one thousand times faster than before humans arrived on the Earth.[160] More than ever, forests, fisheries, and drinking water supplies around the world were all threatened by climate change. Some even took to calling the threat "the sixth extinction," on par with five previous global extinction events, including the one that wiped out the dinosaurs.[161] Perhaps there was a way to protect global biodiversity not only by conserving land at a much greater scale than Wyss had before but also by galvanizing others around the world.

The question was how.

COLLECTING A FEW GOOD IDEAS

Let's say Wyss was prepared to donate $1 billion to protect wildlands and the biodiversity they nurtured—an order-of-magnitude change from the tens or hundreds of millions of dollars he had given previously. To whom should he give that money? What kind of projects would allow him to make the biggest difference? Which efforts would inspire other philanthropists and governments to step up their own conservation plans?

To answer these questions, as was his habit, Wyss began to solicit ideas from experts in the field and trusted confidants. In April 2018, the Wyss Foundation convened a special meeting to solicit ideas relating to conservation and biodiversity that might feed into and help structure a $1 billion campaign. The foundation didn't indicate that it was specifically looking for proposals on how to spend $1 billion. Rather, it invited guests—including representatives of organizations such as The Nature Conservancy, the National Geographic Society, Andes Amazon Fund, and the University of Bern in Switzerland—to come prepared to brainstorm and speak generally about what *they* would do to galvanize the public around the biodiversity crisis if they had significantly more resources. The foundation wanted smart, original thinking, and it hoped that bringing these ideas together would ignite and encourage creative collaboration.

Meeting participants came forward with a variety of ideas: a campaign to raise more global financing for tackling the biodiversity crisis; increased focus on protecting oceans and large, intact landscapes; the development of sustainable ways to conserve land that did more to address the economic needs of local communities. Participants also heard a presentation exploring what the foundation might do to ramp up its own communication efforts in support of a $1 billion campaign. The discussion was lively, and Wyss came away excited to get a project underway.

As a next step, he and others at the foundation asked participants to expand their thinking into more detailed proposals and to present them at the next meeting in July 2018. He hoped the ideas would be concrete and compelling enough that the board would be ready to approve funding.

At the brainstorming session, the participant who had presented ideas for building more global financial support for biodiversity was Brian O'Donnell, former executive director of the Conservation Lands Foundation. Among a suite of potential initiatives, he had advanced the notion of campaigning at the United Nations for formal adoption of a formidable goal: to protect 30 percent of Earth's lands and oceans by 2030.

In preparation for the upcoming meeting, the Wyss Foundation asked O'Donnell to create a proposal that dropped some of his other ideas and focused specifically on developing such a campaign. As Chris Killingsworth (executive vice president of the Wyss Foundation) remembers, "We really encouraged him to focus on a clear campaign for 30x30 because we thought it would be a way to rally the world around something, and it would be achievable, although certainly not straightforward. We thought [that] the board would get behind it and that it would lead to more international financing of conservation."[162]

It was exactly the kind of audacious, global effort that Wyss had become motivated to pursue.

PRESERVING 30 PERCENT OF THE WORLD'S LAND AND OCEANS BY 2030

O'Donnell had become intrigued by the concept of pursuing a 30x30 campaign a couple of years earlier while pondering the planet's biodiversity crisis. The threat to humanity posed by this crisis was every bit as big as that of climate change. And yet the world was neither paying enough attention to the loss of biodiversity nor doing enough to remedy its underlying causes: the overuse and degradation of land and the overfishing of oceans. Conservation campaigns tended to be local, focused on specific places and the species that inhabited them. These campaigns couldn't keep pace with the real estate developers, energy companies, and others that were gobbling up land for development and scooping up sea creatures into their fishing nets.

To fight climate change, 195 world nations had come together in Paris in 2015 to adopt the goal of keeping planetary warming to within two degrees Celsius of preindustrial levels by the end of the twenty-first century. Known as the Paris Agreement, however nonbinding, this goal had galvanized the global public, fueling political discussions and public policy choices. Yet nothing comparable existed for the biodiversity and conservation crisis. In his research, O'Donnell found that the UN had technically adopted goals of saving 17 percent of the planet's land and 10 percent of its oceans. But these targets weren't scientifically based, nor were they particularly inspiring. Further, it appeared that no major conservationist or group had thought to galvanize public support around a single, memorable global biodiversity goal.

"I felt like we had to change the dialogue," O'Donnell says. "We needed a global discussion about the scale of conservation required to create fertile ground for all of those local campaigns to have a chance."[163] O'Donnell's proposal was to give the world a big, ambitious target on which to focus.

In the weeks before the meeting, O'Donnell huddled with Killingsworth and others at the foundation trying to identify what campaign would succeed in getting the world to make a great leap forward in conservation. Realizing that an upcoming United Nations Biodiversity Conference—the 15th Conference of the Parties to the Convention on Biological Diversity (COP15) meeting scheduled for October 2020—would set new ten-year conservation goals, the team decided that the campaign should be focused on getting the nations to formally adopt a large acreage protection goal at the Conference and finance it.

But what should that goal be? In his 2016 book *Half-Earth: Our Planet's Fight for Life*, Harvard evolutionary theorist E. O. Wilson, who was twice awarded the Pulitzer Prize, had argued that the world needed to set aside half the planet's surface—both land and water.[164] An idea that 30 percent of the world's oceans would need to be protected to save them was first proposed in 2016, and other scientists believed that the absolute minimum was 30 percent for both land and ocean. While 30 percent seemed more attainable than 50 percent, it was still an extremely ambitious target given that only about 15 percent of the planet's land and less than 4 percent of its oceans were protected by the mid-2010s.[165]

But all agreed an ambitious goal was needed to galvanize world leaders to change the face of conservation. So, O'Donnell would present to the board a campaign to have the countries at the Conference formally agree to protect 30 percent of the planet by 2030, later known as 30x30. As the foundation understood, seeking to spur action at the United Nations was a departure for both Wyss and O'Donnell. Wyss, of course, had little taste for big bureaucracies, and the UN was one of the biggest and most intractable out there. For his part, although O'Donnell had worked for years on conservation projects, he'd never pursued advocacy on an international stage. While pitching the project, how would he win support from an initial group of core countries? He and his team would have to figure that question out as they went.

At the foundation's July meeting, held again at the bucolic Holland Lake Lodge near Missoula, Montana, O'Donnell and a few others delivered their final pitches for a set of programs that collectively would help structure

Wyss's $1 billion conservation pledge and galvanize others around the world to address the biodiversity crisis. "The board was asking hard questions," O'Donnell remembers. "'How are you really going to make this work? Why 30 percent? If you do get the Convention on Biological Diversity to agree to this, will countries follow up? How much will it really cost? What will you do after the fact to push conservation along in specific countries?'"[166] The questions went on and on—as O'Donnell knew, this was a group that understood how to drive large-scale, foundational change.

Although O'Donnell couldn't answer each question as well as he wished, Wyss and the others still found his proposed 30x30 campaign to be compelling—exactly the kind of high-profile, high-impact campaign that was worthy of their time and resources. This idea might not even work, but given the seriousness of the crisis and the tremendous impact a successful campaign could have, it was worth a try. Wyss and the foundation agreed to move ahead and approve millions of dollars in funding, not just for O'Donnell's campaign but for an accompanying communications initiative on biodiversity that the National Geographic Society, the century-old voice for the natural world and all that's in it, would undertake. Most important, the Wyss Campaign for Nature was approved: a $1 billion commitment (later increased to $1.5 billion) on Wyss's part that would support the 30x30 goals by funding local land protection efforts, building public support for biodiversity and conservation, and funding relevant scientific research.

The Campaign for Nature was a huge commitment, easily the most ambitious of Wyss's decades-long philanthropic career. Yet as Wyss Foundation president Molly McUsic reflects, it remained firmly in keeping with Wyss's long-standing willingness to think and act independently: No major philanthropists were tackling biodiversity at scale. But rather than worry about being the outlier, Wyss didn't hesitate to step up and be the first mover, because he felt that action here was so urgently needed. On the contrary: The fact that biodiversity represented something of a blank slate made the 30x30 idea all the more interesting to him.

"Many funders want to do what other funders are already doing," McUsic says. "What is great about Hansjörg is that he is willing to be the first person. He's always willing to say, 'OK, we should do that.' And he doesn't care whether other people do it or not. That's a fundamental theory of how we function. It is nice to have partners, and ideally others will come along once you have a proof of concept (as happened with 30x30), but it is very important to be willing to go it alone."[167]

"WE HAVE TO SAVE THE PLANET. SO I'M DONATING $1 BILLION."

The Wyss Foundation launched the Wyss Campaign for Nature on October 31, 2018, publicly pledging to spend at least $1 billion over the next decade in support of the 30x30 initiative. Further, the foundation announced that it would fund an initial $48 million round of projects in countries such as Zimbabwe, Australia, Romania, and Costa Rica, conserving ten million acres of land and seventeen thousand square kilometers of ocean.[168] To help draw attention to the urgency of the biodiversity crisis, Wyss took a rare step into the spotlight to announce his support of the global conservation effort, authoring an op-ed in the *New York Times* titled "We Have to Save the Planet. So I'm Donating $1 Billion."[169]

The piece conveyed Wyss's characteristic populism, espousing his dearly held view that "wild lands and waters are best conserved not in private hands, locked behind gates, but as public national parks, wildlife refuges and marine reserves, forever open for everyone to experience and explore." In calling for the world to adopt "the radical, time-tested and profoundly democratic idea of public-land protection that was invented in the United States," he emphasized the role played by local communities in conservation efforts, noting as well the economic benefits that would accrue if people came together to protect wild spaces. All of us, he contended, could play a role in securing our collective future.

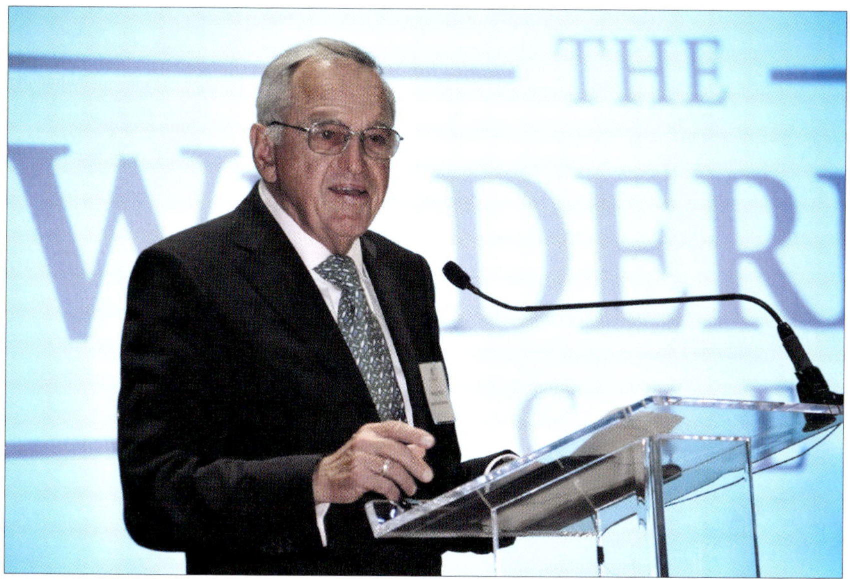

In 2011 Hansjörg Wyss received The Wilderness Society's prestigious Robert Marshall Award for his devoted long-term service to conservation. *(Courtesy of The Wilderness Society)*

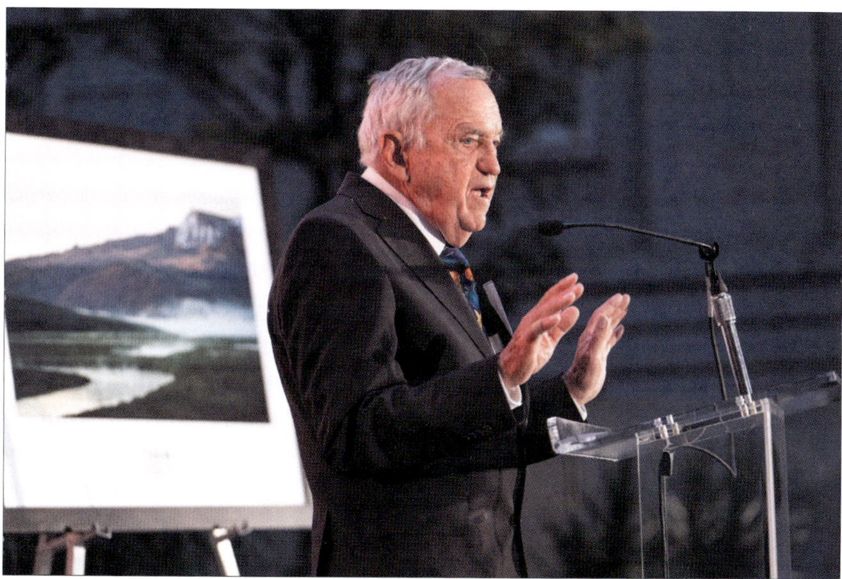

At The Nature Conservancy's 2019 Volunteer Leadership Summit in Washington, DC, Mr. Wyss was honored with a Celebration of Conservation Achievement Award. *(Courtesy of The Nature Conservancy)*

BB

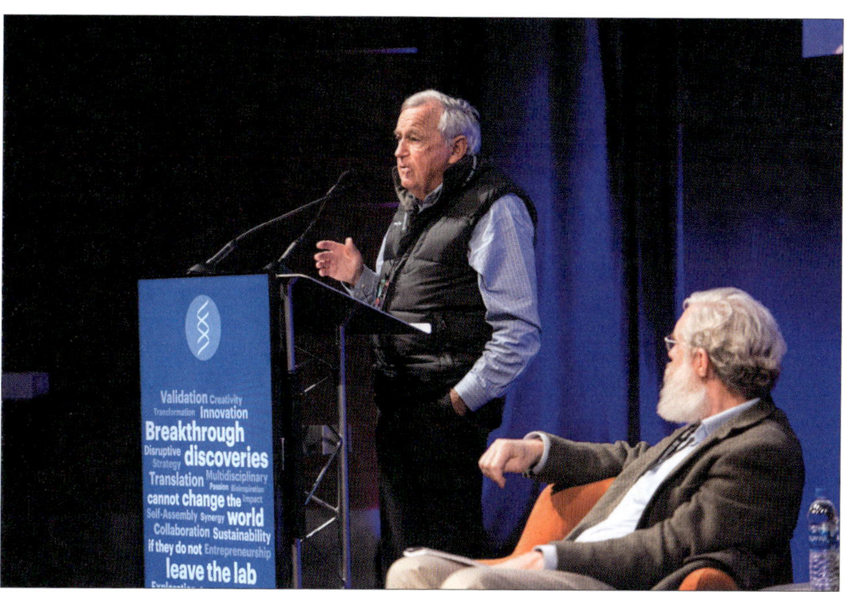

Mr. Wyss, pictured here with Wyss Institute core faculty member Dr. George Church, at the 2019 Wyss Institute for Biologically Inspired Engineering at Harvard University's annual retreat. In an inspiring address, Mr. Wyss encouraged the Wyss Institute community to continue conducting its outstanding research. *(Courtesy of the Wyss Institute at Harvard University)*

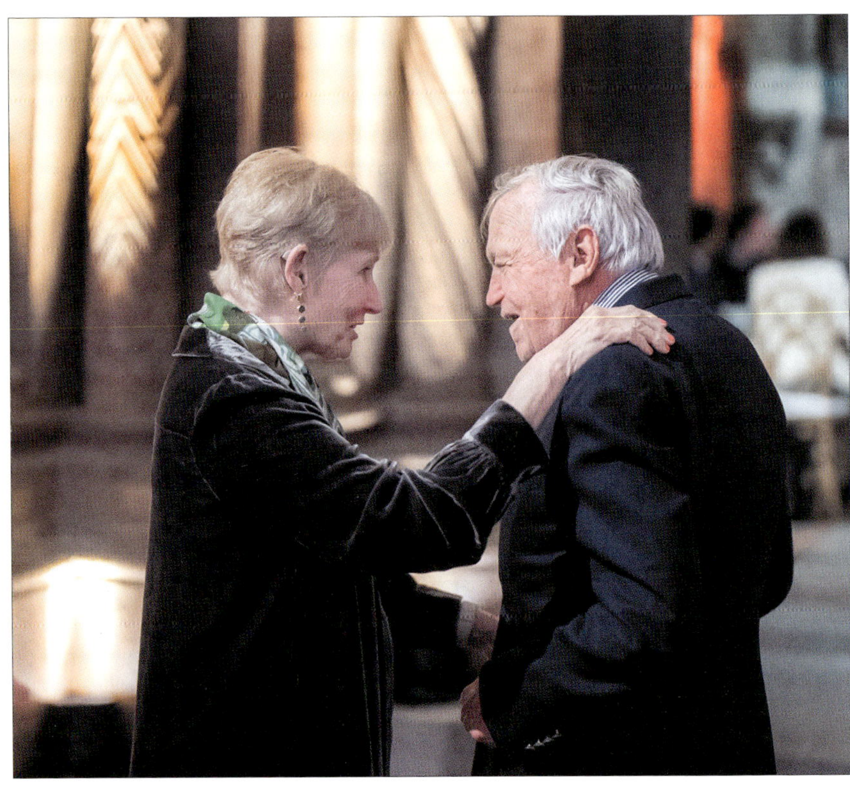

Hansjörg Wyss and his late wife, Rosamund 'Roz' Stone Zander, share a special moment at the 2019 Harvard event honoring his contributions to the Wyss Institute for Biologically Inspired Engineering at Harvard University. *(Courtesy of the Wyss Institute at Harvard University)*

We needed to "see to it that far more of our planet is protected by the people, for the people and for all time."

The article and a press conference Wyss attended drew significant coverage in newspapers around the world, including premier outlets like the *New York Times*, *The Wall Street Journal*, *The Globe and Mail* (Canada), and *Le Matin* (Switzerland). During the week following the launch, social media posts from the Wyss Campaign for Nature received four hundred thousand views. According to Wyss Foundation estimates, some 150 million people on social media saw the announcement of the Wyss Campaign for Nature's creation, thanks in part to posts by the National Geographic Society, a supportive post by the actor and respected environmentalist Leonardo DiCaprio, and messages of support by a number of other prominent groups in the conservation community.

After the launch, the Wyss Foundation began to fund local conservation projects and other initiatives in support of 30x30. Between 2018 and 2022, support from the Wyss Foundation helped to permanently protect almost fifty million acres of land and two million square kilometers of ocean. All told, Wyss so far has committed or spent more than $815 million on land and water conservation around the world in association with the Wyss Campaign for Nature.

Further, as Heath Nero, senior program officer overseeing global conservation at the Wyss Foundation, notes, Wyss's support helped inspire government funding while galvanizing other philanthropists to make large-scale conservation pledges of their own.[170] In 2021, Wyss joined other philanthropists in launching the Protecting Our Planet Challenge, with Wyss committing another $500 million to help the world conserve 30 percent of land and ocean by 2030.

Meanwhile, Brian O'Donnell, with support from the Wyss Foundation, launched the Campaign for Nature, an initiative aimed at securing formal adoption of 30x30 by the United Nations. One of his early moves was to attend COP14, the 2018 UN Biodiversity Conference meeting at Sharm El-Sheikh, Egypt, for a sense of how these big UN meetings worked. O'Donnell found the experience completely disorienting. "You've got all these booths of countries, a lot of microphones with the plaques of countries, and it's just mind-blowing trying to figure out the process and what they're even discussing, the acronyms they're throwing out. And I was like, 'Whoa, what is going on here?' I felt physically lost in this space."[171] Fortunately, O'Donnell happened to stumble upon the Costa Rican booth, and when the staff heard about 30x30, they introduced O'Donnell to Carlos Manuel Rodríguez, the country's environment and energy minister. Rodríguez, a staunch conservationist, was blown away. He offered to serve as O'Donnell's mentor in global advocacy. Costa Rica wound up becoming an early endorser of 30x30, helping O'Donnell forge a strategy and build a coalition of other strong supporters.

When much of the world shut down in 2020, thanks to the global Covid-19 pandemic, COP15 wound up being postponed and played out over time in several different formats and locations. During this delay, O'Donnell and his team did the painstaking work of pursuing individual countries to support formal adoption of the 30x30 target. For each country, O'Donnell compiled scientific research showing how agreeing to a 30 percent conservation goal would impact biodiversity in that country. He laid out how the country could achieve the goal and how conservation could help with other problems, such as reducing the risk of pandemics.

Once travel restrictions were lifted, O'Donnell met with leaders and environmental groups in each country to build coalitions in support of this remarkable goal. With the help of the National Geographic Society and others, he launched on-the-ground media campaigns to build public enthusiasm for conservation and biodiversity. With over two hundred countries to enlist, it was a mountain of work, more than any single person or organization could accomplish alone. As O'Donnell relates, getting it done required building alliances and convincing others to lend their efforts as well.

"Your job is almost evangelical," he says. "You're inspiring someone to then be on your team in a region, in a country—convincing a country to put its diplomatic corps behind this initiative or an organization to work with you on this. So, you're just building coalitions and coalitions."[172]

In the end, all this hard work paid off.

PASSING THE LARGEST HISTORICAL AGREEMENT TO PROTECT LAND AND SEA

At the COP15 meeting, held in December 2022 in Montreal, Canada, nearly two hundred countries formally signed on to the historic 30x30 target. It was the largest agreement to protect the land and sea in world history. Observers called it a "landmark" agreement: For the first time, the world's nations were moving in a concerted way to solve the global biodiversity crisis. It was "a scale of conservation that we haven't seen ever attempted before," as O'Donnell put it.[173]

More broadly, O'Donnell's advocacy with many partners, coupled with the National Geographic Society's communications, succeeded in drawing public attention to the biodiversity crisis, turning 30x30 into the rallying cry the Wyss Foundation had intended. In the United States, President Joe Biden formally proclaimed, upon taking office in 2021, that the United States would commit to the goal of conserving 30 percent of its lands by 2030. And hundreds of state and local leaders across the country signed an open letter affirming support for the national 30x30 goal.[174]

Getting various countries to agree on the goal was the easy part, however. Governments now had to begin following through in order to conserve the land and seas as promised. By late December 2022, governments, philanthropists, and investors had announced annual conservation commitments totaling $8 billion.[175] More than 115 countries had become members of the High Ambition Coalition for Nature and People, a group dedicated to getting the work of 30x30 done.[176] Activist groups continue to apply pressure to governments to set aside more land and ocean for conservation, releasing public letters prior to important global events such as the G20 Heads of State Summit and the African Climate Summit.[177] In practical terms, some countries have managed to conserve more than 30 percent of their land already. Around the globe, by March 2024, about 16 percent of land and about 8 percent of oceans had been conserved so far.[178]

It's unclear how close the world will come to the target, but one thing is certain: If humanity does manage to conserve 30 percent of land and ocean by 2030, or even come close to that figure, it will owe an enormous debt to Hansjörg Wyss. His bold financial support and personal commitment made formal adoption of the 30x30 goal possible, and it inspired many others around the world to join in the fight to preserve wild places.

From O'Donnell's perspective, Wyss's decision to fund the 30x30 campaign helped change the discourse about conservation, transforming the focus on global habitat protection from a relatively obscure discussion in scientific journals to a mainstream global priority. "Hansjörg took the science and put it into action," O'Donnell says. "He took the vision of E. O. Wilson and others and made it possible by funding campaigns and putting resources into it at the necessary scale, and by creating opportunities for other philanthropists and organizations to get into the space. He was, in effect, the tip of the spear."[179] On this issue, the world needed a philanthropist to be a first mover: to think big, step up, and take risks. It needed a philanthropist to lead the way for others. Hansjörg Wyss delivered.

Wyss's success in mobilizing the world around conservation holds lessons for aspiring change-makers everywhere. It affirms key themes examined earlier in this book, including the importance of thinking independently and looking for opportunities that others don't (or can't) see; the usefulness of consulting those around us for insight rather than relying solely on our own thinking; and the virtue of thinking big and aiming for change at scale.

But Wyss's shift to a global scale also suggests a new theme: the importance of constantly challenging ourselves to do more. If we've worked hard on behalf of change and achieved some measure of success, we can run the risk of falling into a state of complacency. It can become harder to set new, more ambitious goals, and more tempting to step back and rely on younger people to innovate and think big. As Wyss's experience suggests, we can and should avoid this trap. Wyss accomplished a great deal as a conservationist before he retired from Synthes, but he made his greatest contributions after that retirement, driven by his restlessness, his sense of duty, and his deep, enduring love of wilderness. Today, he's still pushing himself and others around him to go further. Who knows what he'll do next?

Let's challenge ourselves to keep our past accomplishments in perspective and to push to new levels of success. Let's stay in touch with the passions that inspire us and retain a motivating sense of urgency. Instead of becoming complacent and satisfied, daunted by those things that seem improbable or even impossible, why not set ever more ambitious goals? Thanks in large part to Hansjörg Wyss, thirty is a magic number today in the conservation field. It's up to us to constantly seek out magic numbers as goals of our own, in our areas of interest, and then to do everything in our power to achieve them.

PART III

UNLEASHING INNOVATION AND FIGHTING FOR THE UNDERDOG

10

INNOVATING INNOVATION

Devise pathbreaking solutions not through incremental change in a single discipline but by working across traditional boundaries—and inspire others to do the same.

REVOLUTIONIZING ORTHOPEDIC TREATMENT FOR MILLIONS of patients, saving one hundred million acres of land, and galvanizing countries of the world to conserve 30 percent of Earth's land and oceans by 2030 represent an enormous legacy for any one person to leave. But this is just a portion of what Hansjörg Wyss has accomplished. He also has helped to transform scientific innovation, creating research organizations that have generated hundreds of remarkable, potentially lifesaving innovations—with many more yet to come. And over the past decade, he has funded hundreds of important social justice projects around the world that have touched the lives of millions of impoverished and oppressed people.

Examining Wyss's activity in these two broad areas—scientific innovation (in this chapter) and social justice (in chapter 12)—offers additional lessons that can help change-makers everywhere maximize the good they do.

Another philanthropist interested in unleashing medical innovation to help patients might have been content simply to fund the work of leading scientists who could then achieve dramatic breakthroughs. Not Wyss. The research organization he established at Harvard University in 2009, the Wyss Institute for Biologically Inspired Engineering, represents a whole new model for how scientific innovation takes place in an academic setting. This institute has driven more rapid progress than typical academic departments or research centers, by breaking down both academic silos and the traditional walls that separate the academy from the marketplace. The lesson: We can accomplish more as advocates, activists, and philanthropists if we help others overcome the usual disciplinary and bureaucratic hurdles that so often stifle creativity and innovation.

A NEW KIND OF ACADEMIC RESEARCH ORGANIZATION

The Wyss Institute's story begins in 2005, when Wyss visited Harvard to speak with leading researchers and learn about potential philanthropic opportunities. He already had gifted $25 million to the Harvard Business School to support doctoral education, and he had made smaller gifts to its medical school and art museums.[180] Now he was thinking of making a much larger gift to advance engineering and the sciences.

A traditional approach might have been to set aside funds for the university to build out its engineering department by hiring ten or twenty new senior professors over the next decade or so. But Wyss didn't want the university to do more of what it was already doing in engineering. He wanted to transform the discipline in a way that took advantage of the school's long-standing strength in medicine and the biological sciences. The point, in his mind, was to advance scientific knowledge in a way that brought lifesaving innovations more quickly from the laboratory bench to patients' bedsides.

During his visit, Wyss noticed that while Harvard scientists seemed to be pursuing compelling research questions, they were overly siloed in their approach and failing to engage with ideas in adjacent disciplines. These professors also seemed to be excessively removed from practical concerns, defining success in terms of the acclaim they received from their peers rather than the development of practical innovations that would help people. "Professors worked [toward one intellectual goal], then they gave a speech at a big scientific meeting, la-di-da, nothing ever happened," Wyss says. "They had to work in an environment where they can't just pursue their research. When they're challenged by others, when they have to spend time analyzing and evaluating other projects within the same room and have other people evaluate their projects, I mean, there's a lot of research that's done in isolation."

The problem of intellectual isolation became apparent to Wyss during a lunch meeting at Harvard, when he asked his hosts to tell them about "crazy" ideas they might one day wish to pursue. The conversation moved to astrobiology and the study of molecules found on meteorites that had crashed into Earth. Wyss jumped in, suggesting that if astronomers wanted to gain more insight into life on other planets, they should study these molecules in close collaboration with biologists. "Well, that went over like a lead balloon," Wyss remembers.

He complained to an old friend, Harvard vice provost Howard Stevenson, that they needed to do something to change the dynamic.[181] Stevenson connected Wyss with Steven Hyman, Harvard's provost at the time, who was focused on building up Harvard's relatively small engineering program. Hyman liked Wyss's thinking about interdisciplinary collaboration and agreed to help create a philanthropic opportunity that would excite Wyss. The rough plan was for Wyss to make a major gift to create a new interdisciplinary research institute, and for Harvard to contribute funds as well to show that it was serious and committed to the effort.

Working with Stevenson, Hyman convened a committee of deans and leading faculty in engineering, along with the world-renowned

Boston-area hospitals affiliated with Harvard. The technology these faculty were developing was extraordinary, but as the committee discussed what to do with a major new philanthropic gift, it was clear that they weren't up to the task of reimagining scientific innovation. "Self-interest just showed through everywhere," Hyman says. "Instead of doing something really integrative and really innovative, people were—and not in a cynical way—kind of filling in gaps and holes in their particular school or mini empire. And I knew this would not pass muster with Hansjörg, and it didn't."[182]

Hyman and Stevenson decided to take a different approach. Instead of relying on a committee to generate a novel and exciting idea worthy of Wyss's funding, they enlisted the help of renowned cell biologist Don Ingber, a professor at the medical school, as well as widely respected bioengineering professor Dave Mooney, and directed the committee to serve in an advisory capacity. As Hyman remembers, Ingber was known internally as "an inveterate rule breaker, extremely creative, who bridled at all of the normal institutional constraints."[183] Hyman and Stevenson asked Ingber and Mooney to come up with an idea that would not only cross disciplinary boundaries but disrupt current practices of scientific innovation—a proposal that would anticipate where engineering would be thirty years into the future.

Ingber and Mooney got to work, consulting with faculty members at Harvard and its hospitals as well as at other universities. Drawing on their previous research experiences, Ingber and Mooney began to think in ways that paralleled Wyss's own intuition about breaking down silos. As they observed, scientists in previous decades had transformed medicine and industry by applying engineering principles to solve real-world problems. But in the interim, science had discovered quite a lot about natural mechanisms for building and controlling materials. With this knowledge, scientists and engineers could now move in the reverse direction, starting with biological principles and using those to inspire entirely new ways of solving engineering challenges.

For instance, in trying to come up with a new kind of adhesive, engineers and scientists working together might consider the ways that the footpads of certain lizards stick to surfaces and enable them to walk across ceilings. The point, as Hyman describes it, was to study "what evolution has accomplished, for clues to truly novel solutions."[184] At dinner one night, Ingber came up with a pithy phrase to capture this idea and the purpose behind the new, cross-disciplinary institute that Wyss might wish to fund: "biologically inspired engineering."[185]

Others at Harvard loved this idea, so over a six-month period, Ingber and Mooney drafted a comprehensive business plan to pitch both internally and to Wyss. Ingber recalls being mindful of Wyss's requirement that the new institute focus on delivering real-world impact. "Hansjörg said, and this is a direct quote, 'I know big companies. They basically do incremental advances, and they're not going to do disruptive things. It's like turning a tanker. And I know what you guys in academia do—you do innovative stuff, but you publish papers and nothing ever happens. I want to see the best of both worlds combined here.' And that really reinforced our vision and inspired us to develop a business plan that had some detail to it."[186]

In the broadest sense, the plan Ingber and Mooney developed called for the creation of an independent institute within Harvard that would bring together principal scientific investigators from the university and other Boston-area institutions to collaborate on projects that were so innovative they would not normally receive support from traditional research funders such as government agencies or private foundations. Because the institute would remain within Harvard, it would have access to its world-class faculty and other resources. But because it was independent, it would be able to hire people with backgrounds that Harvard typically didn't seek out, including technical and business development experts from industry. These professionals would team with scientists to develop revolutionary ideas on the frontiers of engineering, science, and medicine that held the potential to change patients' lives.

Instead of simply adopting traditional academic goals like getting more research papers published or bringing in more external research grants, the Wyss Institute for Biologically Inspired Engineering would seek to commercialize its innovations, creating useful products—medical devices, vaccines, diagnostic tests, treatments, and so on—that could be sold either by start-ups spinning off from Harvard or by outside companies that would acquire licenses to these technologies. It's not uncommon for academics to look down on commercialization, seeing it as somehow impure and a corruption of pure science. The Wyss Institute took a different approach, however, regarding the creation of commercially viable products as the best and quickest way to get powerful innovations from the research bench to the patient's bedside.

The business plan not only laid out various research areas that the institute would cover at the outset but also, at Wyss's insistence, specified a series of metrics it would evaluate to track its success. Those metrics included everything from business measures such as the numbers of patents generated to the institute's ability to commercialize new technologies via start-ups, licensing arrangements, and so forth.[187] For Harvard, and indeed most of academia, the emphasis on practical innovation and commercialization was "really, really revolutionary," Hyman says.[188]

Wyss liked the plan's rough outlines, but he didn't commit to it right away, even after Ingber and Mooney made a series of presentations. Instead of granting final approval, Wyss paused the conversation for almost a year and a half. When they reconnected in August 2007, with Ingber pitching the idea yet again to Wyss, he responded positively, but he wanted to be sure of Harvard's commitment to the idea before he would agree to fund it.

In the months that followed, Wyss had Synthes board member (and fellow Harvard grad) Bob Bland meet with Ingber and Mooney to help vet the project. To Ingber's surprise, Bland asked the two professors to create a risk assessment that analyzed the project as well as the factors that might prevent it from succeeding. Ingber had never been expected to create such a document before, but he recalls that the exercise proved hugely valuable, allowing him and Mooney to determine some of the project's administrative details, including the terms of how to structure its governance to ensure autonomy within Harvard. Bland also worked with Ingber and Mooney to pin down budgeting for the institute. Meanwhile, in 2008, Harvard showed its seriousness by contributing seed money to foster some initial scientific collaborations, creating the Harvard Institute for Biologically Inspired Engineering.

In the fall of 2008, Wyss signed a final agreement committing to a $125 million gift over five years—at the time, it was the largest single donation in Harvard's history—to establish the Wyss Institute for Biologically Inspired Engineering.[189] Rather than give an even bigger gift to keep the institute running for a longer period, Wyss preferred to encourage accountability by allocating funds in increments. If the institute lived up to its promise and proved its business model within its first five years, he would make a subsequent gift to extend its longevity—and then repeat the process every five years. The Wyss Institute would have to prove it was making sufficient progress against metrics that related to the commercialization and spread of innovation for patients' benefit, which was Wyss's ultimate goal. He didn't just want effort and original thinking on the part of researchers. He wanted tangible impact. He wanted results.

Upon launching in January 2009, the Wyss Institute brought together fourteen prominent scientists from Harvard, MIT, and Boston-area hospitals as core faculty. These prominent scientists had diverse research interests ranging from cell biology to polymer physics to nanotechnology to robotics to clinical medicine, and the institute gave them both funding and free rein to develop fresh, intriguing ideas. To further enhance cross-disciplinary collaboration, the institute hired several dozen technical experts (engineers and scientists) from industry who had experience translating science into marketable products as well as managing teams.

The institute assigned the technical experts to partner with core faculty to help lead a core set of enabling technology platforms that would focus on bioinspired innovation. Not only did this inject expertise in product development; these experts helped the institute hire others from a range of companies, creating a more dynamic, action-oriented environment where answers to vexing technical challenges might come from unexpected directions. As one academic article on the institute explained, "When one of our scientists raises a medical technology challenge, such as the need for a new material with particular physical properties, the answer might readily come from [a technical expert] who has worked in an entirely different field and has encountered a material with similar properties in a completely different application." These experts, who were well versed in the commercialization of technology, also helped teams at the institute build on promising technologies to create "high-value applications."[190]

Some aspects of the Wyss Institute's structure and workflow were clear at the time of its founding, but many of the details evolved gradually as operations got underway. Mooney had opted out of an administrative role, preferring to focus on his scientific research. But Wyss believed it was vital for Don Ingber, who had played a lead role in helping to conceive the institute, to stay on as its founding director and execute his vision. Ingber felt immediate pressure: "I had this money, and I had to figure out: How do we get this up and running? I had a five-year timeline, so [if I didn't find success,] this would die in five years, with no promises of additional funding."[191]

Over the first several years, Ingber helped the institute develop a novel way of organizing the ongoing work of technological innovation. When researchers or staff members came up with an exciting idea with great potential, they formed teams working within one of the institute's enabling technology platforms (either an existing one or an entirely new one), outfitted with resources that included relevant equipment and technical know-how. Just like the cells that make up the human body, these teams and platforms were "self-organizing, dynamic, and constantly evolving based on the shifting intellectual interests of [the] community members as well as the technical needs and challenges of the wider commercial marketplace."[192] Core faculty had considerable discretion over budgets, so teams moved quickly to pursue pathbreaking ideas without having to jump over endless bureaucratic hurdles. Initially, the platforms focused on areas that, to a layperson, might have seemed straight out of science fiction, including small devices that mimic conditions at the cellular level inside human organs (known as "biomimetic microsystems") and "anticipatory medical devices" that could "sense the threat of injury or the onset of a life-threatening event and stimulate the nerves and muscles in such a way as to prevent it from happening."[193]

As experiments proved successful, the institute continued to fund innovations, sending them down a pipeline of ongoing conceptual development; prototype development; testing and optimization of the prototype; further validation through both technical and commercial de-risking of the technology in response to industry feedback; and potentially, commercialization via spin-out as an independent company or a licensing agreement to an outside commercial partner. Especially promising technologies were refined or validated internally to become as attractive as possible to potential customers and investors, run essentially as virtual start-ups with the help of experienced entrepreneurs-in-residence brought in from outside. All along the funnel, institute researchers collaborated closely with clinicians, on-site intellectual property attorneys, dedicated business development experts, and others to "pursue the shortest path toward developing new technologies that have the greatest chances for commercial success, and hence, the highest likelihood of reaching patients."[194]

Unlike at many outside companies, Wyss Institute teams had the benefit of—and access to—technical equipment at Harvard, as well as at the broad consortium of other academic and medical institutions whose faculty, staff, and students were active at the institute. When technical questions arose, they could easily consult global experts in particular fields who worked at one of these institutions. The funnel process was designed administratively to be both decentralized and agile, devolving as much power as possible to the researchers. The idea was to reduce the bureaucratic barriers that typically impede innovation inside companies and universities, while bringing resources to bear at just the right moments. Ultimately, Ingber conceived of the entire institute operating as one big "start-up in the midst of the world's greatest academic environment."[195]

TRANSFORMING THE DEVELOPMENT OF LIFESAVING MEDICATIONS

For a sense of how the institute's innovative model of cross-disciplinary collaboration worked (and still works) to drive practical innovations, one might consider the case of Dr. Daniel Levner, a young engineering PhD who arrived at the Wyss Institute at the time of its founding. Interested in the intersections between engineering and biology, Levner noticed that an exhilarating, collaborative environment was quickly growing up as the organization took shape. "Right away," he says, "you're exposed to a group doing something in robotics, and a group doing something with DNA, and a group doing something with some interesting chemistry, and so on."[196] At a minimum, the conversations were interesting, but as Levner realized, they also "very frequently yielded collaborations." Levner noticed too that researchers had unusual access to the resources they needed to take novel ideas and run with them. "Where we were missing skills," he explains, "there was almost always somebody at the Wyss Institute we [could] turn to and ask for help or ask for suggestions." His intellectual journey at the Wyss Institute illustrates the serendipitous twists and turns that can occur as experts from specific fields get to know and work creatively with one another.

Levner initially became involved in a project dedicated to helping doctors more easily and rapidly identify bacterial or fungal infections that cause septic shock, a medical condition that can very quickly turn fatal. The hope was to give doctors a new tool that would allow them to determine more reliably whether a patient had sepsis, and if so, which medication they should administer to treat them. The project originated out of casual conversations taking place at the Wyss Institute: A researcher sitting nearby was working on a certain kind of protein that seemed relevant for this application. He and Levner began talking about how Levner's engineering background could help him turn this protein into a useful diagnostic test for doctors. Levner's boss, the renowned Wyss geneticist, molecular engineer, and core faculty member George Church, saw potential in the idea and agreed to let Levner work on it. As Levner realized, the diagnostic test could also potentially incorporate DNA technology that he'd learned about previously as a member of Church's lab.

Levner's diagnostic project fell under Ingber's purview, as the institute's director was also overseeing research efforts around the discovery of the protein that bound the pathogens. And now that Ingber had become acquainted with Levner, he called him in to consult on a different project: the development of instrumentation to enable culturing of human "organ-on-a-chip" microdevices. Ingber's team had begun work on these artificial devices that mimic human organs in part because every year, over one hundred million animals die as a result of their use in medical and scientific experimentation in the United States alone.[197] To make matters worse, given the differences between animal and human biology, animal subjects often don't produce the best, most reliable test results, leading to extensive failures in clinical trials. Instead of using animals for testing, what if we could perform testing on the artificial organs? With this technology, could scientists run experiments that would allow them to better understand disease processes and develop new ways of treating them?

Ingber and his colleagues had been working for years on this device: a small wafer containing a microenvironment (made of actual human cells) that recreates conditions present in the lungs, heart, brain, and other organs.[198] After publishing a seminal paper on the technology in 2010, Ingber asked Levner to help write a proposal for funding from the US government's Defense Advanced Research Projects Agency (DARPA).

With DARPA's support, Ingber's team could develop an instrument for integrating chips for multiple organs into a model that mimics the human body—a human "body-on-chips"—and in turn develop this technology into a marketable product.

The proposal was successful, and $37 million in funding was approved. Starting in 2012, Ingber enlisted Levner to take charge of the engineering side of the project. Over the next few years, the organ-on-a-chip team grew to about forty people who continued to experiment with the technology and ultimately filed over two dozen patents. In engineering a commercial product, the team drew on technical, industry-related insights from Wyss Institute experts to design prototypes in ways that the pharmaceutical industry would find helpful and relevant, thus increasing the odds that the product would have value in the wider world. The team pursued several collaborations with pharmaceutical companies, using the prototypes to help solve specific technical challenges these companies were having. The experience not only helped researchers at the Wyss Institute further define and refine prototypes but also established their technology's commercial viability for potential investors.

In 2014, responding to pressure from pharmaceutical companies eager to use the technology in more significant ways, the Wyss Institute spun out a start-up called Emulate to produce and market the innovation. Nineteen members of the team dedicated to the project left to join Emulate, reflecting the natural flow of talent in and out of the institute. Among those who left was Levner, who became Emulate's cofounder and chief technology officer.

Over the next several years, Emulate continued to develop its products, raising over $200 million across five rounds of investor funding and launching its first product in beta form in 2017. Today, the company continues to grow, selling a range of products and services based on the organ-on-a-chip technology to customers that include twenty-four of the twenty-five leading pharmaceutical and biotechnology companies.

Emulate's commercial success is good news for medical research, because it means that research will ultimately improve the lives of patients. As Levner describes it, as organ-on-a-chip technology works to achieve the worthy goal of saving the lives of laboratory animals, it should also allow for "much more correct, more predictive assessments of new compounds to see if they'll be safe and effective in humans."[199] In helping pharmaceutical companies do their work better, "the real target is making [available] better drugs, safer drugs, and more efficacious drugs that are potentially also cheaper."

For Levner, the significance of the Wyss Institute's new model of technology innovation was clear. Without the institute, bringing the technology to market would have been a far slower process, and it might even have remained stuck forever in a lab. The institute "really permitted us to come out strong with a good technology and a patent portfolio with good funding, with a good idea of what the market needs."[200]

AN ENTIRELY NEW MODEL FOR DISRUPTIVE INNOVATION

The Emulate journey is just one success story among many at the Wyss Institute. Since 2009, research from the institute has led to almost 3,000 scientific publications, more than 4,250 patents filed, and nearly 1,500 patents issued. The institute has spawned fifty-eight start-ups that collectively have received over $2.2 billion in venture funding while creating more than 1,800 jobs.[201] Today, the Wyss Institute accounts for about 20 to 25 percent of all patents and start-ups created at Harvard University each year—a truly staggering record of success.

Proud of the institute's progress, Wyss philanthropies have continued to provide financial support, making additional donations since the organization's founding of $125 million in 2013, $131 million in 2019, and most recently, a pledge of $350 million in 2022. The payoff from these investments has been extraordinary. In effect, an investment from Wyss has unlocked billions of dollars in additional funding, unleashing a tidal wave of innovation while enhancing the Boston area's stature as a hub of biomedical innovation. Perhaps most impressive of all is the creation of a whole new ecosystem of start-ups whose technologies promise to advance medical science that saves and improves many lives as well as technologies that can help to combat climate change—all in less than fifteen years.

Yet the numbers alone don't fully convey the impact of the innovations that the institute has cultivated. So far, Wyss Institute teams and start-ups have licensed or sold technologies that prevent infants from developing sleep apnea, repair damaged eardrums, turn greenhouse gases into ingredients used in food production, prevent cancer, and uncover therapies for complex diseases more quickly, to name just a few. And the future seems just as promising, as researchers work on "biological suspended animation" that maintains organs in dormant states outside of the body for extended periods of time; a new kind of air conditioning that is much more energy efficient and environmentally friendly; and 3-D printing technology to create artificial organs with blood vessels that doctors can use to help reconstruct women's breasts following surgery for cancer. Institute teams are also creating new diagnostic tests for Lyme disease, new immunotherapies for cancer, and new ways of treating fungal infections. They're developing new ways to deliver medications to the brain—a challenge that, if solved, would enhance the treatment of brain disorders like Alzheimer's. They're creating molecules that can be programmed to build themselves, so doctors might one day deploy "molecular robots" inside the body to diagnose and treat illness at the molecular level.[202]

Beyond these innovations, the Wyss Institute's most far-reaching contribution may be the new, more collaborative model of development it has pioneered. "We thought we were going to develop an institute, to create bioinspired materials and devices," Ingber says. "In the end, we developed an entirely new model for disruptive innovation." Ingber takes pride in the institute's profound impact within Harvard, proving that it's possible to accelerate progress if we "break down barriers between disciplines, between departments, between schools, between institutions"—and between academia and industry. Other programs at the university have cropped up to support entrepreneurship, reflecting a recognition that to achieve real-world impact, science can and should be pushed beyond the academic tower and into the marketplace.

Ingber continues to receive calls and visits from academic institutions, governments, and companies around the world eager to learn about the Wyss Institute and borrow some of its structures and practices.[203] Ultimately, Wyss's support for the institute is, as former Harvard president Lawrence S. Bacow has said, "a gift . . . to all of the academy . . . because it has helped us to understand how we can organize these institutions to make them even more effective." The institute serves "as a model for how other institutions can have an influence on the world."[204]

Looking back on the Wyss Institute's history, Steve Hyman gives Wyss an enormous amount of credit for having "this vision for a very different kind of organization that would be at the borders between engineering, science, and medicine . . . that would sit within Harvard, have access to all its faculty and all its resources, but would also have a great deal of independence." It was Wyss's vision, Hyman suggests, that led the institute to hire people in areas like project management and business development, who had never before been hired at Harvard. The result was a great success, to the point where "there are probably a number of other institutions doing experiments that are very much inspired by this Wyss model."[205]

Wyss's experience with the Wyss Institute for Biologically Inspired Engineering illustrates several of the action principles that he embodies, which were explored earlier in this book: Adopt a critical mindset to spot hidden opportunities. Stay true to your sense of purpose (which, for Wyss, has always revolved around helping people). Cultivate a pragmatic, results-oriented mindset. Pursue change at the greatest scale possible. But these key principles all point us toward another one: Challenge the boundaries, categories, and silos that underpin our lives and our work, and empower others to do the same. Maintaining a pragmatic mindset and questioning the status quo will lead us in short order to test boundaries with an eye toward groundbreaking results and to push ourselves and others beyond those that seem illogical and impede progress. Meanwhile, for change-makers, a desire to achieve lofty goals at scale will provide us with the motivation to push against powerful forces that are invested in maintaining the traditional silos.

Some progress can result from playing it safe and keeping conventional boundaries intact. But as the old saying goes, a ship in port is safe, but that's not what ships are built for. Solving the biggest challenges in an expeditious way requires flexibility, creativity, innovation, and collaboration at higher levels than traditional boundaries typically can accommodate. As many artists, entrepreneurs, and other creatives will attest, only through willingness to venture outside familiar terrain and make ourselves and others uncomfortable can we open up new horizons of possibility. Who knows what might be possible if we look more readily to adjacent disciplines and cultivate more cross-disciplinary partnerships? As Hansjörg Wyss has often said, and as the experience of the Wyss Institute so far confirms, "When talented, creative people are given the freedom to work together across disciplines, there are few problems they cannot solve."

11

FOUND IN TRANSLATION

Think imaginatively about how you might translate effective approaches or techniques to solve additional problems elsewhere.

IF HUMANITY MANAGES TO save Earth in the decades to come, some of the credit might well owe to the humble Brazil nut. This long, meaty nut, whose shape somewhat resembles an oversize garlic clove, comes from the *Bertholletia excelsa* tree, which grows naturally in the Amazon rainforest.[206] Although people in Western countries have been eating these nuts for centuries, their popularity has lagged far behind other varieties, such as peanuts or almonds.[207] More recently, Brazil nuts have generated more interest, with some experts suggesting that their large stores of the nutrient selenium, an essential mineral, might help keep our thyroid healthy and our diabetes in check.[208] Studies have found that eating Brazil nuts can promote health via multiple pathways, including by improving how the cardiovascular system functions.[209]

You can't grow these nuts well in commercial megafarms. Rather, you must harvest them from wild trees in the rainforest. So what's good for consumers might also turn out to benefit the ecologically threatened areas where Brazil nuts are grown, most notably the Madre de Dios in southeastern Peru, a richly biodiverse forest that comprises 15 percent of the Peruvian Amazon.[210] Much of this region remains pristine, but despite the formal granting of protected status to large swaths of land, significant deforestation due to illegal logging has occurred. Brazil nuts might play a role in keeping further deforestation under control in the years to come, if we can find a way to help local populations improve their livelihood by developing new products using Brazil nuts and structuring supply chains so that they can extract more value from nut production.[211] With a strong economic incentive to protect the living rainforests where Brazil nut trees grow, local populations will be more likely to make sure legally protected areas stay intact.

The challenge of protecting land over the long term is what scholars have called a "wicked problem," one that is rife with complexities, paradoxes, and tradeoffs, defying a clear or simple solution.[212] "If you don't address the conflicts and underlying causes" of such problems, says Peter Messerli, director of the Wyss Academy for Nature at the University of Bern, "you'll have to defend [the land] with fences and weapons. If we don't change the way we produce food or how we make our economy work in certain countries, then we can ultimately not protect it."[213] That's why, as Messerli explains, although legal protections such as those described in this book are vital, they'll prove meaningless if poverty and inequality among local populations goes unaddressed.

Social and political pressures can lead such communities to exploit land destructively, regardless of its protected status. So the Wyss Academy, headquartered in Bern, Switzerland, has been developing Brazil nuts as a market-based solution that can help local communities thrive while also reducing economic pressure on biologically sensitive lands. It's part of the academy's broader, more integrative approach to conservation. In addition to organizing and facilitating Brazil nut production, the academy is testing out other innovative solutions that reconcile conservation with economic development, including ecotourism: bringing tourists to local farms. "It is so important to show that people can make a living from the forest and improve their lives without cutting down the rainforest," says Miguel Saravia, who directs the Wyss Academy's efforts in South America. "Without such efforts, the trees will be in danger."[214]

If you haven't heard much about solutions such as these, that's because little work of this kind is being done. Scientists have raised the alarm about the challenges posed by climate change and advocated for science-based measures like carbon credit schemes or more sustainable agricultural techniques, but they haven't done much to translate these measures into practical, grassroots solutions for preventing nature's degradation in distressed areas. Meanwhile, the policymakers charged with implementation have tended to work from a distance, imposing these solutions simplistically onto local communities. Lasting progress requires new, integrative solutions that are tailored to the social and economic needs of local populations, and further, that are devised and implemented with local participation. Scientists must venture out of their cloistered labs and team with policymakers as well as groups and individuals in imperiled areas around the world.

It's precisely this novel kind of engagement between scientists, policy experts, and local populations that the Wyss Academy for Nature seeks to nurture. Founded in 2018 with funding from Hansjörg Wyss, the Canton of Bern, and the University of Bern, the academy is focused on "developing, testing, and scaling up innovative solutions that advance nature conservation and human well-being at the same time."[215] The academy meets that aspiration by convening a unique combination of "researchers, diplomats, entrepreneurs and innovators collaborating with the business community, policymakers, civil society, and communities to cocreate strategies and practical results."[216]

If the idea of a pioneering organization aimed at practical, cross-disciplinary innovation sounds familiar, that's because it is the same approach discussed in the previous chapter. The Wyss Academy for Nature takes the model that Hansjörg Wyss helped pioneer at Harvard and adapts it to the challenge of land conservation. Whereas the Wyss Institute for Biologically Inspired Engineering sought to turn pure science into marketable products that doctors or patients can use, the Wyss Academy for Nature's goal is to create new, grassroots policy solutions that bring clear benefit to local communities while preserving natural spaces.

There's a lesson here for aspiring change-makers: As admirable as it is to experiment with novel ideas, it's not nearly enough. When those ideas wind up bearing fruit, we must think imaginatively about how to deploy them in new contexts. Working within a discipline to solve a problem is important, but we can make more progress if we operate across domains, lifting what works in one area and shifting it to drive positive change elsewhere. Ideas might not translate perfectly, but if we're open to it, lifting and shifting might extend an insight that can yield double or triple the impact we initially imagined.

TWO MORE TRANSLATIONS OF A GOOD IDEA

To gain a fuller picture of how Wyss translated the innovation of Harvard's Wyss Institute for maximal effect, let's leave conservation for a moment and return to the world of medical innovation. The creation of the Wyss Academy for Nature followed closely behind two other new medical innovation accelerators created by Wyss on the model of Harvard's Institute. The first of these organizations was the Wyss Center for Bio and Neuroengineering in Geneva, Switzerland.

In 2012, Wyss received an email from Patrick Aebischer, then president of a leading Swiss technical university, the École Polytechnique Fédérale de Lausanne (EPFL). Having visited the Wyss Institute at Harvard, Aebischer expressed his enthusiasm for what he'd seen and asked whether Wyss might be interested in partnering on something similar in Switzerland. Wyss responded positively, and the two began imagining what this center might look like. Wyss felt drawn to the idea of a translational research organization focused on neuroengineering. From what he could tell as a nonspecialist, patients hadn't seen much benefit from recent advances in the study of the brain. Treatments for brain-related conditions like hearing loss or macular degeneration hadn't progressed very much, which presented an important opportunity for Wyss to make a difference. "I like to bring positive change," Wyss told the audience at a 2015 conference on philanthropy and brain science. "If we can get something from the lab . . . into the hands of industry and disseminate it to patients who need to be cured . . . then that's the kind of change I want to bring."[217]

One important matter to resolve was where this center would be located. Eager to preserve the center's autonomy, Wyss insisted that it not be situated on the EPFL campus or at any other area university. A unique opportunity soon presented itself when, in 2012, the pharmaceutical giant Merck put up for sale its large, state-of-the-art building in the old industrial district on the shores of Lake Geneva. Wyss, along with the Swiss businessman and philanthropist Ernesto Silvio Maurizio Bertarelli, bought the building the following year to house the new Wyss Center, which was founded in 2014 as part of a gift Wyss made of $105 million.[218] As Aebischer remarked, locating the Wyss Center on such "neutral ground" forced interactions across the usual disciplinary boundaries, creating "a different environment than the usual environment"—one that no doubt was more dynamic and innovative.[219]

As has often been the case in his conservation philanthropy, Wyss saw an opportunity to maximize his philanthropic impact by partnering with others and leveraging their contributions to achieve more than he could on his own. In occupying space in the former Merck building, the Wyss Center for Bio and Neuroengineering anchored a larger research hub called Campus Biotech, created by Wyss and Bertarelli in partnership with EPFL and the University of Geneva. The idea was to create a new technology and innovation ecosystem in Europe akin to those in the United States, such as Silicon Valley or the Route 128 tech corridor in the Boston area. Campus Biotech is focused on three areas of interest: neuroscience, global health, and digital health. In addition to the Wyss Center, the hub includes the Geneva School of Engineering, Architecture and Landscape (HEPIA), the University Hospitals of Geneva (HUG), and the Swiss Institute of Bioinformatics (SIB) as well as various start-ups and established companies.[220] As "a unique ecosystem that brings scientific platforms [and] academic, clinical, industrial and entrepreneurial actors together"—one that also seeks to effect "a transition from academic research into industry-driven development"—the hub reflects the vision animating the Wyss Center itself.[221]

Like the Wyss Institute, the Wyss Center is working on important medical advances that in some cases seem to verge on science fiction. One project is a breakthrough brain-computer interface called ABILITY that doctors can implant in patients who are "locked in" their bodies due to illness or injury. In preclinical trials as of 2022, ABILITY would allow stroke patients to grasp objects or move around, and would help patients with amyotrophic lateral sclerosis (ALS)—a progressive neurodegenerative disease that attacks nerve cells in the brain and spinal cord, also known as Lou Gehrig's disease, for a popular baseball player who died from ALS—to communicate with the outside world.[222] Other projects include developing a new approach to studying brain tumors, using gene therapy to help patients recover from devastating spinal cord injuries, creating software that can spot dementia at earlier stages than is possible with current technology, and building new kinds of neural implants that doctors can use to treat epilepsy and other conditions.[223] To ensure that such work continues, Wyss in 2022 made an additional grant of approximately $110 million.

Geneva isn't the only site in Switzerland that now has an innovative, cross-disciplinary institution funded by Wyss. In 2014, two professors at Zurich-based universities—Roland Siegwart, a specialist on robotics at the Federal Institute of Technology Zurich (ETH Zurich), and regenerative medicine expert Simon P. Hoerstrup of the University of Zurich—approached Wyss for help supporting research into an innovative technique that extracted portions of liver from sick patients, grew the liver in a lab, and then reimplanted the liver.[224] By allowing patients to serve as their own liver donors, the technique promised to get them off of transplant waiting lists and potentially save their lives. These discussions led to a bigger idea: the creation of a new center that would bring the two universities together, with an eye toward transforming advancements like the liver technique and other scientific breakthroughs into clinically usable products. The center would fund research projects that other investors typically ignore because the time required to bring them to fruition is too long.[225]

Wyss was receptive, in part because he had earned his engineering degree from ETH Zurich and wanted to give back to the institution. He also saw an important opportunity to close the gap on a glaring lack of collaboration between the two institutions. Incredibly, the faculty at the two schools had little to do with one another, even though they were physically located only about a tenth of a mile away from one another. Researchers at the University of Zurich were doing excellent basic research. But lacking insights from their engineering colleagues at ETH, their discoveries weren't turning into products that could help patients.

In late 2014, Wyss contributed $120 million to create the Wyss Translational Center Zurich, an institution that aimed to "accelerate the development and application of innovative medical therapies and groundbreaking robotic systems."[226] The center's initial projects, developed across the two platforms of regenerative medicine and robotics, included the liver research (called Liver4Life) as well as artificial blood vessels and other tissues that can grow and heal themselves; improved artificial heart replacement for patients waiting for a donated organ; and a system that serves as artificial eyes that might help vehicles navigate better in real-life situations.

This work has proved extremely fruitful. As of 2023, the Liver4Life team had accomplished the first-ever implant of a lab-regenerated liver into a patient, with the patient "doing well" a year after the procedure.[227]

The Wyss Translational Center Zurich also has given rise to a number of exciting start-ups that are bringing medical advances to the market: The Zurich Eye helps robots see the way humans do. Hylomorph's products reduce complications that patients frequently experience with devices implanted surgically into the body. Hemotune uses nanotechnology to treat patients by removing substances from the blood. Seervision is a system that integrates artificial intelligence with cameras to more easily and naturally capture videos of in-person presentations. And denovoSkin offers "personalized, bio-engineered, dermo-epidermal skin grafts."[228] A diverse set of other great projects underway includes development of a new kind of underwater drone, a personalized treatment for repairing muscle tissue, and a treatment for colon cancer that activates bacteria inside the gut to bolster the patient's immune system response. All told, the Wyss Translational Center Zurich has advanced twenty-five projects that collectively have created over 650 jobs. In 2022, Wyss affirmed his commitment by making a new gift of approximately $130 million.

A NEW APPROACH TO CONSERVATION

In the wake of the Wyss Translational Center Zurich's establishment, administrators at the University of Bern wondered whether Wyss, the city's hometown kid, would be interested in investing in scientific research there as he had in other Swiss cities and in the United States. They approached Wyss with an idea of their own for an institution that would foster cross-disciplinary work with real-world impact. Instead of focusing on a given area of medicine, however, they proposed a project in the environmental space that would bring together experts in three disciplines where the university had particular expertise: sustainable land use, climate science, and biodiversity.

In 2018, Wyss agreed to hear a formal presentation by Peter Messerli and other University of Bern professors. As Messerli recalls, the professors spoke about the need to bring these normally siloed fields together to enhance efforts in sustainable development. The bonds between these fields were critically important, they told Wyss. Grasping the global biodiversity threat and the threat of a sixth extinction meant understanding climate science, and climate mitigation couldn't take place without transforming land use at a time when the Intergovernmental Panel on Climate Change at the United Nations estimates that current land use practices—from agriculture to deforestation—are responsible for nearly a quarter of human-caused greenhouse gas emissions.[229] By creating innovative connections across the three fields, the new center envisioned by the University of Bern professors would make economic development more sustainable.

Wyss responded well to this argument, but he had two concerns. First, he hadn't heard the professors talk about concrete solutions. Messerli remembers Wyss saying, "I don't want just another research institution telling us how complicated and disastrous the world is. I want solutions."[230] Second, Wyss didn't wish to fund abstract scientific work conducted solely in Europe. He wanted work that was happening in the field, particularly in places like South America and Africa, where he was funding other philanthropic work. He invited the professors to refine their pitch and present it to him again. If they could correct for these two issues, he might agree to fund them.

During the months that followed, the professors continued to work on their idea and to connect with Wyss when they could. Eventually, the professors' pitch was refined enough that Wyss judged it ready for presentation to the board of the Wyss Foundation. The board's response was decidedly mixed. There might be potential for a new kind of cross-disciplinary center in the conservation world, they thought, but the proposal was still too conceptual. How would the center actually deliver a significant impact? The board offered the professors a grant of 2 million Swiss francs (about $2.2 million) to spend the next year or so developing pilot projects in Africa and South America, in order to prove the concept behind the proposed new academic center.[231] If they could return at the end of this trial period with a more robust proposal, and if they could find matching funds from other organizations, the project would be approved.

The Bern team succeeded on both counts, and in December 2019 the Wyss Academy for Nature was launched at the University of Bern with a pledge for 100 million Swiss francs from the Wyss Foundation. Matching funds—50 million Swiss francs each—came from the Canton of Bern and the University of Bern. A portion of the Canton of Bern's contribution went to fund projects on the ground that, in the words of the cantonal government's president, would "show that economic development is reconcilable with the protection of nature in a comparatively highly developed region like the Canton of Bern."[232]

In addition to Switzerland, the Wyss Academy for Nature maintained regional hubs in Southeast Asia, East Africa, and Latin America, where interdisciplinary teams of experts would run experimental programs designed to balance economic development and sustainability. As part of its work during its first five years, the academy has functioned much like a start-up incubator, developing and running seven experimental programs at its hubs, including the project involving Brazil nuts in Peru. Unlike conventional nongovernmental organizations operating with public money, the academy would have a mandate to experiment with breakthrough concepts that held promise but might carry a greater risk of failure than other projects—the research equivalent of "go big or go home."

But as Messerli clarifies, the academy doesn't only test innovative ideas; it also combines existing ideas in promising new ways. "You have many NGOs that are doing things," he says. "But bringing these cogwheels into clockwork where they interact and reinforce each other—I think that's the big space of innovation where [the global community] is failing and that we can really support with science."[233] It's also, as the East Africa hub director Benson Okita argues, a chance to practice a more holistic approach to conservation, "by being aware of the needs of the human communities whose buy-in is essential for the long-term success of ensuring nature's resilience."[234]

As of 2022, the Wyss Academy for Nature had approximately eighty projects underway across its four hubs.[235] In Kenya, the academy worked with the local population to build infrastructure that can hold reserves of water to sustain economic activity during periods of drought. In Laos, the academy embarked on a pilot project to plant trees in cornfields with the hope of weaning local populations away from exploiting forested areas.[236] In Bern, the academy fielded a project that tested sustainable vegetable production and another that promoted the use of recycled concrete in construction—part of a plan to help fuel a more sustainable, circular economy.[237] And the academy's efforts to develop the indigenous Brazil nut industry in Peru have been successful and well received by the local population so far. With the encouragement of the Peruvian government, the academy is working to determine whether this program might be scaled across the country to other protected areas, or expanded so that local populations can make and sell products made with Brazil nuts, such as a popular yogurt made from the nut's milk.[238]

As the Wyss Academy for Nature uncovers "concrete pathways toward mutual benefits between nature and people," it looks for connections between them, aiming to create "systemic feedback loops between these interventions to expedite the transition toward a shared and evidence-based vision."[239] Translated, that means the academy spreads the notion of a new relationship between local populations and the environment that surrounds them, by connecting with stakeholders around the world, including scientists, public policy experts, and activists and other practitioners on the ground. Over the long term, the academy seeks to spread best practices for attacking the "wicked problem" of achieving sustainable economic development. Peter Messerli believes strongly that "the gap between knowing and doing is getting wider and wider" when it comes to conservation,[240] and to counteract this and inspire future progress, the academy is taking action while teaching in the process. It's challenging work that proceeds slowly, but it might be the best—or even the only—path toward ensuring healthy ecosystems around the world, as well as healthy, thriving communities, over the long term.

The work of the Wyss Academy for Nature is grounded in a crucial idea: that while our lives on this planet may be fragmented, there is much to be gained by knitting the parts back together into a cohesive whole—to reconcile nature and human prosperity, as well as local communities and abstract scientific knowledge. Like the other three innovative scholarly organizations Wyss has helped to create, the academy does the valuable work of translating across boundaries to make that kind of reconciliation possible, whether it's bridging the chasms between academic disciplines or the ones between theory and practice.

This approach challenges the rest of us to likewise integrate our own lives as change-makers. When we find a technique or a model that works in one field, geographic location, or type of organization we care about, why not try to apply it to others? Hansjörg Wyss dares and inspires us to be multifaceted individuals with many diverse interests and to think nimbly and creatively across our own self-created boundaries, translating insights and approaches for the sake of progress.

As the saying goes, a great deal is lost in translation. But quite a bit of practical know-how is found as well.

12

THE "BRANDING IRON IN YOUR BRAIN" APPROACH TO GIVING

Direct your energies and resources by looking inward, focusing on areas that feel personally significant and enduring.

IN CITIES AND TOWNS across America, you'll find kind, thoughtful, dedicated individuals advocating at the street level for society's underdogs. Elise Johansen, executive director of a nonprofit organization called Safe Voices, is one of them. Founded in 1977, Safe Voices is a domestic abuse and sex trafficking resource center serving three under-resourced rural counties in Maine, including the poorest square mile in New England outside of Boston. With a staff of about thirty and a 2023 budget of $3 million, the organization operates a 24/7 emergency helpline that helps abuse survivors gain access to resources and strategize how best to stay safe or escape harmful situations.[241] Safe Voices also provides longer-term, personalized advocacy for individual survivors; offers emergency housing; runs support groups; and administers a domestic violence intervention program that educates batterers and provides them with the critical knowledge they need to make different choices and avoid abusive behavior.

The work performed by Safe Voices staffers is emotionally taxing. In a given week, they might help a woman escape a boyfriend who held a knife to her throat and threatened to kill her. They might counsel a woman trapped in a living situation with an alcoholic spouse, advising her on how to stay as safe as possible during future abusive encounters. They might assist a nonbinary victim in navigating the bureaucracy required to obtain restraining orders. They might help a male victim rent a new apartment by getting him the thirty-five dollars he needs to obtain the state ID a landlord requires as part of a rental application.

Over the past five years, demand for the services provided by Safe Voices has jumped by over 40 percent. Like many other forgotten places in the United States, particularly in the wake of the Covid-19 pandemic, these Maine counties have experienced a mental health crisis as well as a rise in homelessness and opioid addiction, all of which have led to an increase in sex trafficking and abuse. An ongoing housing crisis has made life more difficult for the victims of trafficking and abuse by making it extraordinarily difficult for them to escape harmful domestic situations. Although desperate to escape, they often have nowhere to go.

Although Safe Voices receives substantial public funding, it doesn't come close to covering the costs of its programming, much less allow the organization to provide better compensation for its dedicated staff while making needed long-term improvements. To keep the lights on and strengthen the organization, Johansen must rely heavily on the generosity of philanthropists. And that's where Hansjörg Wyss comes in.

One day in 2015, while going through the mail, Johansen's predecessor found a check for $30,000 from the Wyss Foundation. At the time, Safe Voices had an annual budget of only $1.1 million, so $30,000 represented quite a significant gift. It came as a total surprise; Safe Voices staff didn't have a previous relationship with Wyss or even know who he was. The surprise continued the next year when a check showed up again—and the year after that, and the year after that. Wyss Foundation money gave the organization an enormous boost, comprising one of its larger sources of nongovernmental support. Unlike other philanthropic gifts, Wyss's giving was one of the few that arrived consistently, year after year. Although a one-time gift can help pay for programming, a consistent annual gift allows Johansen to include that money in the budgeting process and make longer-term investments, including increases in pay to retain dedicated and talented staff. As she affirms, the impact of Wyss's gift has been tremendous—so much so that she has reached out to the foundation to express her gratitude. "How do I say thank you?" she asks. "Because this is huge for us, and the impact is gigantic, and I feel like I want to tell him."[242]

Today, even after so many years of receiving checks from the Wyss Foundation, Johansen and her team remain surprised. Wyss is most widely known for his conservation-related philanthropy, especially his $1 billion commitment to the Wyss Campaign for Nature. What was he doing supporting a small organization like Safe Voices in an out-of-the-way corner of Maine? "We don't know why he chose us," says Grace Kendall, Safe Voices' director of development and engagement. "He really mostly focuses on land conservation."[243]

While that observation may be true, Wyss's donations to Safe Voices were no fluke. Wyss in recent years has supported an army of organizations that provide services or advocacy on behalf of or by women, including women experiencing domestic abuse. These include, among others, Abby's House in Worcester, Massachusetts; the Elizabeth Stone House in Roxbury, Massachusetts; PeaceWomen Across the Globe, a Swiss-based "feminist peace organization"; and Rosie's Place (billed as the nation's first women's shelter) and the Women's Lunch Place, both in Boston, Massachusetts.[244]

The Wyss Medical Foundation, established in 2009 and focused on addressing health disparities globally, has funded many other programs that address women's health around the world. One of them is Seed Global Health, an NGO that seeks to improve health in less developed countries, in part through programs dedicated to improving maternal and child health. The organization helps to create a "pipeline of midwives, nurses, and obstetricians who advance access to respectful, high-quality care for 15 million expecting mothers and children" in four African countries.[245] The Wyss Medical Foundation also supports Global Action in Nursing (GAIN), which helps to make childbirth safer in Malawi, Sierra Leone, and Liberia by providing training and mentoring to nurses.[246]

Wyss has a deep, lifelong concern for women's health and welfare. Switzerland during his youth was a culturally conservative society that adhered strictly to traditional religious teachings. Even into the 1970s, Swiss women couldn't vote and enjoyed little autonomy in their economic affairs, unable even to open a bank account without their husband's consent. Such patriarchy seemed to Wyss a gross injustice. It "upset me a great deal," he says. "I was very upset. Really, physically—it made me mad."

Wyss's concern for women's health was shaped by his mother, who was an iconoclast when it came to gender relations. It was the norm for housewives in his family's neighborhood to hang sheets out on the balconies to dry during the morning hours, but as he recalls, his mother often refused, preferring to read a book instead. And after lunch each day, which she prepared, she insisted that his father clean up while she read the newspaper. "If the neighborhood would have known, they would have called the police. She was already very different. My parents were totally different from my friends' parents, really."

Wyss's mother became politically active, marching in support of women's voting rights, which Swiss women finally gained in 1971. Wyss remembers being astonished at the ridiculous things Swiss politicians said in their efforts to keep women out of politics. "They were the craziest arguments," he says. "The most important meal in many Swiss families is Sunday lunch. And the politicians said, 'Well, there will be no good Sunday lunch because the women will have to go and vote.'" At an early age, such arguments led him to reject those who would diminish women and deny them the same opportunities as men, including control over their well-being. "You grow up with these arguments," he says, "and it stays like a branding iron in your brain." Decades later, he is still doing his part to fight oppression and lift up women.

That long-standing commitment is worth pondering. Our world is so troubled that it can be hard for well-meaning, socially minded people to know how to direct their energies. With so many diverse challenges to address, where should one even begin? Once you've begun to engage as an activist or a philanthropist, it's easy to become distracted as new causes emerge to compete for your attention, potentially diminishing your impact. Wyss's support for women-related causes and social justice causes in general reflects an intentional approach in which change-makers remain focused on their most deeply held beliefs and stay close to their roots. In Wyss's case, his philanthropy has had so much impact because it isn't trendy, superficial, or abstract—it's deeply personal, and thus enduring.

GOING BIG *AND* BROAD

Following the 2012 sale of Synthes and Wyss's retirement from the business, the new financial resources at his disposal enabled him to expand his giving in new directions. Wyss had already magnified his commitment to making a difference so it swelled beyond his key passion of conservation. He had made his first, important gift to the Wyss Institute for Biologically Inspired Engineering at Harvard, but well before that, he also had made many small, targeted donations to other causes that interested him, from advancing women's health and welfare to promoting social justice to supporting medical science and the arts, all while continuing to direct the vast majority of his giving toward conservation.

After the former bank CEO Herb Sandler, Wyss's friend and fellow philanthropist, urged him in 2009 to broaden his impact beyond conservation, Wyss started contributing more to champion these issues. By 2011, he was giving to a wide array of organizations, ranging from the *New York Times*' Neediest Cases Fund, the National Women's Law Center, and the Mexican American Legal Defense Fund to Planned Parenthood, the Museum of Fine Arts Bern, and the Association of Arizona Food Banks.[247] Some of these donations amounted to just a few thousand dollars, while others were in the millions.

Wyss's interest in these disparate areas was just as personal and enduring as his concern for women. Ask him, for instance, why he wants to help the underserved, and he seems almost baffled at the question. The impulse to relieve the suffering of the less fortunate is so deeply ingrained in him as to seem obvious or self-evident, beyond what words can convey. "I can't answer that question," he says. "I don't know. Somebody comes to me and says this is an area that really needs help and needs health care, I can't answer why. I like to help people there, and that's it."

Looking back on his life, it is easy to speculate about the potential origins of Wyss's desire to help those who lack resources and privilege. It seems reasonable to trace it back to his modest upbringing in Switzerland, which left him generally identifying with everyday working-class people instead of the privileged and powerful. Although he didn't personally experience poverty, racism, or gender discrimination, he internalized a set of traditional middle-class values rooted in helping the less fortunate while doing your part to make the world a better place. His actions at Synthes revealed his belief that business executives have a duty to care about the welfare of their lowest-paid employees, who deserve to benefit when they help build something. More broadly, Wyss feels that the more wealth you possess, the greater your responsibility to look out for society's underdogs, doing whatever you can to help them flourish. It is common sense to him—and a matter of common decency—that the very privileged should help those who are in need.

Wyss also has a long-standing interest in supporting the arts, a passion he got from his father, who was a mechanical calculator salesman by profession but also a passionate artist. His father exposed him to the hobbies of drawing and painting early on, taking him to museums and creating small pictures for Wyss's mother, pasting them into books he bought her. "He made a dragonfly for her, or he drew a funny clown who gave a flower to a good-looking lady under a tree. He painted all kinds of things," Wyss remembers fondly. Wyss cultivated an early love of music, too, singing at school as a boy and later, while working as an usher at a Bern concert hall, enjoying concerts given by Arthur Rubinstein and other famous classical musicians. While in his forties and leading Synthes, he took up clarinet for a time, taking lessons and practicing for hours each week.

These varied experiences led Wyss to collect art and listen to music later in life, while also inspiring him to share his affinity for the arts with others. In his view, the creation of and interaction with art isn't always a comforting experience, but it's one that can expand the human mind, just as going out into nature and seeing a magnificent sunset can. "It's so important that young kids see that there's something else, other than football games on TV or dumb shows—that actually somebody sat down and painted something."

In 2012, Wyss again pondered how to expand his giving. As always, he wanted to make sure that he was deploying his resources to the greatest effect. Leaders at the Wyss Foundation solicited help from a consultant, who came back with a number of intriguing ideas about how Wyss should approach philanthropy beyond conservation. The foundation, for instance, could undertake a major campaign to help people in developing countries buy stoves. Or it could create a signature initiative to support community colleges and apprentice programs. Or it could lead a high-profile effort to improve fisheries around the world. The suggestion that raised the most eyebrows was the idea that the foundation should take on rare diseases, from river diseases to elephantiasis. "These weren't bad ideas at all," Wyss Foundation president Molly McUsic recalls. "All of them were really interesting."[248] But ultimately, Wyss just couldn't get excited about them. If he was going to expand the breadth of his giving, he believed that he would have the biggest impact addressing needs where he felt the greatest personal connection and passion. Women's welfare and social justice "needed help and interested me," he asserts. "I didn't want to jump on something else I didn't know anything about or have enthusiasm for."

Wyss thanked the consultant for his thoughtful ideas but chose to follow the causes that most moved him and motivated him at his core. The Wyss Foundation would still largely focus on conservation, of course, but it would look for new opportunities to invest in women's issues, social justice, the arts, and medical research. In 2016, at Wyss's prompting, the foundation further refined and clarified the areas in which it intended to pursue philanthropy over the next ten years, coalescing around four key goals: global conservation, economic security, women's equality, and democracy. The decision was made to handle Wyss's contributions in the arts and medicine/health separately for the most part (the latter arriving via the Wyss Medical Foundation), and likewise for the funding of his research institutes. Although this general division of labor persists, the Wyss Foundation today continues to make some grants in the arts and medicine/health as well as to Wyss's research institutes.

Wyss and McUsic also took steps to ensure that the foundation would remain as small, nimble, and efficient as possible, even as its staffing levels and contribution amounts increased. Instead of adopting formal budgets that would induce specific levels of potentially wasteful spending, the Wyss Foundation invested opportunistically as good ideas presented themselves. The foundation continued to keep a low profile, insisting (as any great organization does) that the credit was due to its grantees, which were doing the actual work. It also eschewed forms of bureaucracy that would slow it down and reduce its effectiveness.

"A lot of foundations have bureaucracies on top of bureaucracies, have too much staff, are not very efficient," Wyss says. "I wanted to have a foundation that was very efficient and where the staff had a lot of leeway to propose and approve projects."

INCALCULABLE IMPACT

With this plan in place, the Wyss Foundation and the Wyss Medical Foundation have had an enormous impact in recent years. Beyond his work supporting women's health and welfare, Wyss has driven a considerable amount of philanthropy to organizations that support underserved or marginalized populations both in the United States and abroad, including refugees, those lacking proper housing, and those without proper access to medical care.

In addition to GAIN and Seed, Wyss has been a major funder of the AO Alliance, an outgrowth of the AO Foundation, whose programs aim to improve care for trauma-related injuries in over two dozen low- and middle-income countries. Similarly, as the next chapter reveals, the Wyss Wellness Center provides a range of basic health and wellness services to refugees and immigrants in Philadelphia.[249] Wyss has also made large gifts to help patients in the United States who can't afford quality care: A $15 million gift to NYU Langone Health gives uninsured patients access to restorative plastic surgery, while a $5 million gift to Children's Hospital of Los Angeles provides needy children with access to orthopedic surgery regardless of their financial status.[250]

The extent of Wyss's support for society's underdogs is so far-reaching and diverse as to be almost dizzying. He has supported many small, local initiatives designed to provide resources to those who need it, including the Chester County, Pennsylvania, food bank; Carriage Town Ministries in Flint, Michigan; the Daemion Counseling Center in Berwyn, Pennsylvania; the Jackson Cupboard in Jackson, Wyoming; Mobile Meals of Southern Arizona; and Meals on Wheels in Kingsport, Tennessee, among others. He also has sought to engage on the level of public policy, funding organizations dedicated to advancing equity in society, such as the Center on Budget and Policy Priorities, which focuses on giving all Americans access to basic human needs (education, health care, housing, and so on), and the Constitutional Accountability Center, a think tank that seeks to protect the rights of underserved and marginalized groups through legal advocacy and scholarship.[251] Other Wyss-supported organizations include the National Health Law Program, which intervenes legally to expand access to health care; the Washington Center for Equitable Growth, which supports economic policies that broaden prosperity in the United States; and Georgetown University Center for Children and Families, which "conducts research and offers solutions to reduce inequities and improve the health of America's children and families, particularly those with low and moderate incomes."[252]

The impact of Wyss's giving—both through his foundations and through his own personal philanthropy—is incalculable. Consider just one organization that has received funding from Wyss personally: the AO Alliance.

Each year, 4.4 million people, many in underserved nations, die from orthopedic injuries they have suffered, simply because they don't receive proper treatment. The big-picture economic damage from such injuries is extraordinary, costing low- and middle-income countries some $180 billion in lost productivity.[253] These countries often lack the medical infrastructure and skilled caregivers required to properly treat bone fractures, which are so routine in developed nations, and few NGOs are helping to address the problem. The AO Alliance was formed to fill that gap while reducing, in its words, "suffering, disability, and poverty."[254] In 2022, it trained over 6,500 caregivers in more than thirty countries in Asia and Sub-Saharan Africa. The AO Alliance also has engaged comprehensively in specific countries like Malawi, Ethiopia, and Ghana, creating training courses while supporting the health-care infrastructure. Although the need remains great, since 2015, the AO Alliance's work has improved the lives of thousands of injured patients by hosting more than 1,200 in-person learning events, training over 40,000 health-care workers, and sponsoring nearly 550 medical fellowships as of early 2024.[255]

Other organizations Wyss supports also are making an important impact. With funding from the Wyss Foundation, the Children's Hospital of Los Angeles's Jackie and Gene Autry Orthopedic Center was able to hire sixteen new team members. In 2022–2023, these team members treated almost six thousand patients on an outpatient basis and over four hundred in the hospital, almost all of whom came from underserved families. According to Alex Carter, the hospital's senior vice president and chief development officer, this was a "huge impact" that allowed the hospital to see patients it otherwise wouldn't have the capacity to serve. In the absence of Wyss's gift, these children would have either received lower-quality care at an adult hospital or waited much longer to be treated.[256]

Kimberly Baltzell, who leads the GAIN program at University of California San Francisco (UCSF), proudly recounts that thanks to support from the Wyss Medical Foundation, her program has provided long-term mentorship and training to over four hundred nurses and midwives in three African countries. As a result of the program, one site in Liberia reported a 60 percent drop in cases of women giving birth to stillborn babies. In a local area in Malawi, data showed a substantial increase in caregivers' ability to recognize several major and potentially fatal childbirth complications.[257] Other localities have seen similarly dramatic improvements.

In the arts, one of the biggest stories in Wyss's philanthropy has been his support of the world-renowned Fondation Beyeler in Switzerland. For years, Wyss purchased works of art from the organization's founder, one of the world's foremost dealers of modern art—the late Swiss art dealer Ernst Beyeler—nurturing a long friendship with him. "I just liked him as a person," Wyss recalls. "He was just a nice man. You know what I mean? He came by bicycle to work—an old bicycle. He was down-to-earth. He was just somebody you love to be in company with."

During the 1990s, Wyss donated $25 million to help Beyeler's foundation build a museum to make Beyeler's awe-inspiring private art collection—including paintings and sculptures—open to the public. There is a reason the Fondation Beyeler is one of the most visited art museums in Switzerland: With Wyss serving as chairman of the board, the museum strives not merely to present important works but to make them relevant, especially to young people. "Many museums still have high intellectual barriers," senior curator Ulf Küster says. "They have to learn that this has to change. And the big advantage of our museum is that Ernst Beyeler [and] Hansjörg Wyss know exactly that a museum is not an ivory tower anymore—certainly not our museum."[258] Located in a parklike natural setting that has the feeling of a refuge, the museum has been visited by over seven million people since its founding in 1997.[259] In 2021, the Wyss Foundation announced a $72.5 million grant to build a major expansion to the museum. According to Sam Keller, director of the Fondation Beyeler, the gift would "help the institution to fulfill its mission to bring art to a broad public for generations to come."[260]

When it comes to the formidable impact they have on people's lives, the smaller, more modest, less visible organizations on Wyss's list of grantees are just as noteworthy as the larger ones. Take Safe Voices, the domestic violence resource center in Maine. Grace Kendall was present at the organization's main offices one day when a woman came in urgently seeking help. Unlike most clients who ring the doorbell and wait for a staffer to let them in, this woman rapped on the door a couple of times—a sign to staffers that she felt a powerful sense of immediate danger and a fear of being physically harmed. As the woman began to tell her story through a flood of tears, the desperation in her voice was evident. This woman "was not safe, and she knew it," Kendall says.

Kendall's colleague ushered the woman into her office and closed the door for a private conversation that lasted about forty-five minutes. Kendall doesn't know what they discussed, but when her colleague's office door opened again and the woman emerged, her disposition was entirely different. She had a smile on her face and sweetly thanked Kendall's colleague, saying, "I feel like I know what's next." The woman's situation hadn't changed, but a trained advocate had listened to her story and strategized with her about handling her abuser so she could stay safe. Her suffering had eased, and she was in a better position to take some measure of control over her life.

After the woman left, Grace and others in the office went over to their colleague to compliment her on her efforts. "Do you see what you just did here?" they said to her. "You took this woman who was panicking and desperate and really hopeless, and she left able to say, 'I know what to do next.'" And in that moment, all of them broke down in tears. As enormous as the problem of domestic violence is, and as hard and necessary as their daily work continues to be, the impact they are having on their community is palpable. They are making a difference, changing their clients' lives for the better.

There isn't space in this chapter to describe all that Hansjörg Wyss has done to impact women's issues, social justice, and the arts. Suffice it to say that Wyss magnified his impact by meeting the needs and pursuing the causes that were most personal to him, year after year. What can other change-makers take away from Wyss's example? Don't feel like you need to solve every problem. And don't shift your focus constantly, glomming on to the latest cause du jour before moving on to something else. The way to drive the most lasting impact is by applying sustained effort in a few selected areas that matter most to you.

Take a moment to think back on your life. Consider the injustices or suffering you saw unfolding around you as a child—the unfair things that bothered you the most. Reflect on the areas of engagement that have long seemed most urgent to you, that most align with the values you hold dear. What remains with *you* like a branding iron in your brain? If more people were to adopt Wyss's humble and passionate focus, applying whatever resources are at their disposal, they might be more likely to pursue their good works over the long term. Their impact on the world would undoubtedly be extraordinary.

13

THE POWER OF BEING CHOOSY

Carefully vet opportunities for change, and have the courage to say no before finding your way to yes. Make windmills tilt toward you.

DURING THE MID-2010S, STEVE Schwartz, director of the Wyss Medical Foundation, engaged in a series of discussions with Dr. Alexander R. Vaccaro, a distinguished spine surgeon who is president of the Rothman Orthopedic Institute, a world leader in its field, and teaches at Thomas Jefferson University in Philadelphia. Vaccaro wondered if Wyss might be interested in supporting the creation of a center of excellence in the field of degenerative disk disease of the spine. The two fleshed out the idea, with Schwartz providing feedback and Vaccaro coming back with multiple iterations of a proposal.

Schwartz appreciated the work that Vaccaro was putting in, but as time passed, he sensed that the idea didn't seem right for Wyss.

Degenerative disk disease is a serious condition that affects millions and can cause crippling pain. If anyone had the capability to do good work in this area, it was Vaccaro and his distinguished team. But Schwartz knew that Wyss wanted to help humanity not simply by curing disease but by addressing the serious disparities in health care between those who have resources and those who fall short. Vaccaro's proposal, as attractive as it was, didn't help the underserved to the extent that Wyss typically preferred.

Vaccaro agreed, and he kindly put Schwartz in touch with others at Thomas Jefferson University who might have more suitable projects. That's how Schwartz met a young primary care physician named Marc Altshuler, who in 2007 had begun partnering with a local agency charged with helping Philadelphia-area refugees resettle into new lives. As Altshuler discovered, the need for medical care among this population was enormous, beyond what he'd imagined. The average immigrant in Philadelphia had to wait four months for their first doctor's appointment, even though they had government-funded health benefits for only eight months.[261] That delay often prevented recent immigrants from fulfilling the medical prerequisites required to get jobs and enroll their children in school.

To boost their capacity, Altshuler and his colleagues created the Jefferson Center for Refugee and Immigrant Health, where they saw refugees in the university clinic during designated times each week. The center was soon caring for between three hundred and four hundred refugees per year—more than any other provider in Pennsylvania. And yet even that endeavor didn't satisfy the need within the community. Altshuler responded by reaching out to other academic medical centers in the area to set up clinics there, eventually forming the Philadelphia Refugee Health Collaborative. "When you heard the stories of what these individuals went through, you just knew you had to [help them]," Altshuler says.[262] As a result of these efforts, Philadelphia became the first city in the country where the great majority of refugees went to academic medical centers for their care rather than public health clinics. The Centers for Disease Control and Prevention soon designated the Jefferson Center for Refugee Health as a Center of Excellence for Newcomer Health.

By 2018, Altshuler confronted another realization: Although refugees in the city were receiving appropriate care, a much larger population of recent immigrants remained underserved. The solution, Altshuler thought, was to create a freestanding health and wellness center to care for anyone who identified as an immigrant, regardless of whether they were documented or had health insurance. After creating a business plan to sharpen this idea, he made a formal pitch to Schwartz, who in turn took the proposal back to Wyss. Three months later, Altshuler had his answer: The Wyss Foundation would contribute $3.1 million toward construction of a dedicated facility to provide health care to immigrants. The foundation would later contribute an additional $1 million to help offset additional costs that arose during the pandemic.

As Schwartz anticipated, many aspects of the project appealed strongly to Wyss. Most important, Wyss liked how Altshuler envisioned a center that would fill an important gap by providing vital care to the underserved. "Our philosophy is that health care is a human right, not a privilege," Schwartz says. "These people were underserved—fearful migrants and asylum seekers—and nobody was giving them the resources that they needed. Jefferson was taking care of them, but it didn't have the resources or the space. Wyss was determined to give them both."[263]

Altshuler conceived of the health and wellness center as a place through which medical residents could rotate as part of their training. This feature struck Wyss as vitally important, as it would allow more young physicians to understand community health-care needs, while exposing them to the unique perspectives of the immigrant population. Altshuler also pitched the center as a place that would not only allow for visits with a primary care provider but also provide for a variety of medical, social, and educational needs that are unique to immigrants—which made sense to Wyss as a way to maximize impact. Finally, Altshuler and his team were fully focused on good works, quietly doing their jobs without seeking praise from others. "I think Wyss fell in love with the place just because of the vibe, the feel," Schwartz says.

In April 2021, the Wyss Wellness Center opened its doors in Southeast Philadelphia, an area of the city that is home to many immigrants.[264] In designing the 6,500-square-foot facility, Altshuler and his team met with representatives of a dozen different ethnic groups to understand their needs. Wyss's funding was essential to unlocking smaller gifts from other funders that helped get the center off the ground. "Without his gift, this would not have started," Altshuler says.[265]

Because Wyss stepped up, Philadelphia's refugees and immigrants now have a place to help them take care of a variety of health needs, from vaccines to maternal health. Partnering with a leading social services agency that ministers to immigrants, the Wyss Wellness Center offers patients access to cultural and educational resources without having to leave the neighborhood where many of them live. That's critically important, Altshuler says, noting, "If you want to address the disparities that patients face, you have to bring health care into the communities and not make the communities come to the health-care provider."[266]

Wyss observes that the Wyss Wellness Center has "had a bigger impact than I'd dreamed of," bringing care to a population that desperately needed it. During its first year, the center saw more than 1,700 patients, including many Afghans who had fled the Taliban's takeover of their country following the American military's withdrawal.[267] By June 2023, more than three thousand patients from almost three dozen countries had visited the center, almost 80 percent of whom either lacked insurance or were on Medicaid.[268] "The Wyss Center provides a 'safe space' for patients who might not have anywhere else to go," Altshuler says. "We offer services on a sliding fee scale and have on-site social workers that help patients determine their insurance eligibility."[269] Immigrants in need don't get turned away, as they might elsewhere. The center is always there for them. And as Altshuler notes, that gives them hope. Simply seeing that others care about their well-being made an important difference for the local immigrant community.

One grateful patient is Fatana Bayat, who fled the Taliban with her husband in October 2022. When she arrived in Philadelphia the following year, she was five months pregnant and sought prenatal care at the Wyss Wellness Center. Subsequently, she got a job there as a community health worker, interacting with patients and helping them to get the care and other services they need. Bayat has found a sense of home and belonging at the center alongside colleagues who display tremendous care and professionalism. Helping others transition more easily to American life and secure basic necessities and access to mental health services has been fulfilling for her. "You feel like the Wyss Center is your mom," she says. "You ask everything, and she will provide everything. It's the best definition I can give—that Wyss is like a mom for everyone."[270]

In its first two years of operation, the Wyss Wellness Center already has shown an ability to meet the changing needs of the population it serves. The Covid-19 pandemic provides a good example. Weeks after the center opened in 2021, a vaccine for the virus became available, but patients found it difficult to obtain their shots because, like many recent immigrants, many of them weren't computer savvy and couldn't speak English. Working with Philadelphia's health department, the center secured a grant to host a mobile vaccine clinic at its facility two days a week, open to patients as well as members of the general community. "The word really got out to the immigrant community," Altshuler said, and in nearly a year's time the center dispensed about seven thousand vaccines.[271] In 2022, the center also pivoted in real time to provide care to refugees from Ukraine who were resettling in Philadelphia after fleeing Russia's unconscionable invasion of their country.

As the story of the Wyss Wellness Center suggests, intervening in ways that maximize impact isn't always a straightforward, linear process. Endless opportunities arise to do good in the world, but they might not be the right ones given your interests, concerns, and abilities. To drive real and lasting change, you must be as intentional as possible, staying clear in your mind about both the problems you want to help solve and the types of projects that will put your resources to their most elevated, impactful use. You must then vet potential projects carefully, bypassing needs that, however worthy, don't meet your criteria well enough—and approving those that do. Throughout your change-making efforts, you can realize the most progress by pushing yourself to be choosy, even if this means turning down projects on occasion that are worthy in many respects but not quite right for you.

SEVEN GUIDELINES FOR DRIVING CHANGE

Ask Wyss how he vets projects, and his initial response makes it seem like he doesn't dwell too much on the dilemma and simply goes with his gut. "You get projects that hit you immediately in a most positive way," he says. "Other projects make no sense at all, and then I say no. My enthusiasm changes from project to project. I don't need much thinking or philosophy or anything." But Wyss then goes on to observe that the Wyss Foundation often approves projects opportunistically—for instance, if it trusts the people making the request or admires the work an organization is doing. Ultimately, the foundation's decisions are bounded only by a healthy dose of "common sense and clear thinking," Wyss continues. "It's about impact—how can we bring positive change to other people." As Heath Nero, the foundation's senior program officer in charge of global conservation, puts it, Wyss "doesn't want to tilt at windmills for the rest of time. He wants to get some stuff done, and we at the foundation want [that] too."[272]

But what exactly does Wyss mean by "common sense and clear thinking" when he's talking about philanthropy? Digging a little deeper, we find that Wyss's criteria for vetting projects are quite thoughtful and well developed, tying back to his hard-earned reputation for pragmatism. Over the years, leaders at the Wyss Foundation have distilled his approach into a series of basic guidelines that help to inform decision-making across the foundation's and Wyss's grant-making.

First, projects must be *high impact*. In the case of conservation, that means the land being protected must be large, wild, and intact, and it must contain carbon stocks. In medicine and health, it means that projects must make a palpable difference in the lives of people who are underserved. In all areas, it means that any funds the foundation allocates must bring about measurable change without supporting unnecessary bureaucracy.

Projects also must have a *lasting impact* and must be *feasible within a reasonable time frame*. They should *leverage other funding* when possible. The organizations or individuals proposing the projects should be *good and trusted partners*, and the project should have a *solid exit strategy*—it shouldn't be open-ended. Finally, projects should *respect and protect local communities*. On conservation projects, this can mean safeguarding or even expanding the sovereignty and rights of Indigenous peoples.

When it comes to medical projects, it means not trying to impose solutions, and (for example) instead respecting a country's ability to run its own health-care system.

Seven Pragmatic Guidelines for Driving Change

1. Big impact
2. Enduring impact
3. Feasible in a reasonable amount of time
4. Leverage other funders, if possible
5. Good and trusted partners
6. Existence of an exit strategy
7. Protect and respect local communities

The Wyss Foundation keeps these guidelines front and center for every decision and doesn't hesitate to enforce them. In cases where Wyss sees potential in a project, often he'll ask the individuals pitching it to refine their proposal to make it more impactful, efficient, or practical, as in the evolution of the vision behind the Wyss Academy for Nature at the University of Bern. Wyss also doesn't hesitate to turn projects down when they don't seem entirely aligned with these guidelines, despite otherwise admirable goals (as with the very worthy proposal from the Rothman Orthopedic Institute). As Wyss explains, "I look at each project quite objectively."

Wyss's pragmatic, impact-oriented approach to vetting projects also helps to shape how the Wyss Foundation administers grants. Some philanthropists might be content to write checks and simply assume that grantees are spending their money well, but not Wyss. He requires accountability and the discipline that this engenders, and he infuses that accountability into projects by doling out funds in tranches rather than all at once, and then looking for results. If an organization has made satisfactory progress after a given period, its funding might be extended. Major grantees at the Wyss Foundation and the Wyss Medical Foundation understand that Wyss requires regular reporting. "I think it's clear that he's very interested in [return on investment] and bringing somewhat of a business-type approach to his philanthropic giving," says Dr. Jason B. Anari, of Children's Hospital of Philadelphia's Wyss/Campbell Center for Thoracic Insufficiency Syndrome. "And I'm guessing that this probably has helped to ensure the level of impact that all of his giving has had. It's not just, 'Here's some money,' but 'What have you achieved with it?'"[273]

SEEKING OUT OPPORTUNITY

Being choosy and deliberative about projects doesn't simply mean vetting the opportunities and demanding accountability. Nor does it mean waiting for worthy projects to come to you. If you have a clear sense of what you wish to accomplish, you can proactively seek out opportunities to make a difference. Hansjörg Wyss does this all the time, relying on his colleagues at the Wyss Foundation and the Wyss Medical Foundation to serve as his eyes and ears.

Kimberly Baltzell, professor in the School of Nursing and Health Professions at UCSF, was in Malawi in 2016 when local partners invited her to a remote district in the country that was seeing too many deaths and other negative outcomes among women giving birth. In the United States, women often decorate nurseries and have gender reveal parties before giving birth, fully confident that their babies will survive. But in this corner of Malawi and places like it, they often don't name their children for a few days for fear that they might not live. Since nurses and midwives with limited support were responsible for most of the births in remote areas, Baltzell, along with UCSF and Malawian colleagues, began devising an intervention to help nurses and midwives better identify and treat the worst complications that mothers and babies experience during childbirth. As part of this intervention, local expert midwives would provide regular, long-term mentorship to nurses and midwives after their training (much like an internship for new physicians), helping them to apply the lessons learned to real-life situations. Baltzell and her colleagues ran this intervention as a pilot program, calling it Global Action in Nursing (GAIN).

In 2018, while attending a dinner party, Baltzell struck up a conversation with Steve Schwartz, who happened to be sitting next to her. The two discussed Baltzell's work, and in particular her conviction that frontline personnel often get overlooked in global health, to the detriment of those being served. To her surprise, Schwartz showed interest. Toward the end of the evening, he asked if she would jot down her thoughts about GAIN for him—nothing too detailed, just some language articulating what she dreamed a full-fledged program based on her concept might look like.

Baltzell came back with a brief proposal for a five-year, $14 million expansion of GAIN's pilot in Malawi that would bring it to Liberia and Sierra Leone, two of the most difficult places in the world to give birth, where Baltzell also happened to have partners on the ground. Over the next year, Baltzell kept talking with Schwartz and the Wyss Medical Foundation, refining aspects of the proposal. And then one day in 2019, she received the news: Hansjörg Wyss had decided to commit $2.5 million to fund the first two years of her project, with the possibility of extending it for the remaining three years if it showed sufficient progress. Recalling that moment, Baltzell says, "I honestly could have fallen over, because you think this was a dinner party and I was just chatting with someone, and [yet] they were interested in what I was doing."[274]

It's often easy, Baltzell says, to convince a philanthropist to fund something sexy, like the latest high-tech intervention. But it's much harder to convince them to simply help support and grow the number of nurses and midwives on the ground, even though an adequate number of well-trained health providers can have an enormous impact with the right resources. Schwartz and Wyss had been able to see that promise. Unbeknownst to Baltzell, they were on the lookout for projects precisely like hers: those that would help the underserved; would make a big, tangible difference; and would empower people in the local community rather than simply imposing a solution from the Western world.

So far, Schwartz's and Wyss's opportunity-spotting has paid off. Since 2019, GAIN has expanded in Malawi, entered Liberia and Sierra Leone, and tested its model in the United States (Memphis, Tennessee). In addition to providing nurses and midwives with on-the-job training and long-term bedside support by expert mentors, the organization has awarded scholarships to help students enter the nursing field. The results, as we've seen, have included "reductions in stillbirth rates, better outcomes for women suffering from post-partum hemorrhage," and more.[275] In 2022, the Wyss Medical Foundation renewed GAIN's funding, allowing the organization to continue training nurses and to study the impact its programming is having on local communities.

Wyss's funding of another program relating to health-care equity, Seed Global Health, also reflects opportunity-spotting on the part of his colleagues. Dr. Vanessa Kerry, the organization's founder and CEO, recalls working in Africa as a medical student and realizing that there weren't enough trained doctors or other skilled health professionals to care for patients, a gap that was contributing to poor health outcomes in less resourced countries. On one occasion, she had to deliver a baby herself with the aid of a nurse because a doctor was nowhere to be found. Although Kerry was sufficiently trained, she was only a student and still not fully equipped to help delivering mothers. Recognizing how deeply entrenched such health inequities were, she and her colleagues started Seed to partner with local communities and support the training of health-care providers in local areas.

Kerry didn't come to the Wyss Medical Foundation seeking philanthropic dollars. Rather, the foundation found her. In 2018, Kerry gave a talk about her work at Massachusetts General Hospital, and Steve Schwartz was in the audience. He approached her afterward and asked for more information, to see if any opportunities existed to support her organization. That began a conversation that led to a gift. Wyss committed to multiyear funding that was subject to renewal from year to year, allowing for sufficient accountability. The timing of this gift was fortuitous. For the previous five years, Seed had partnered with the US government's Peace Corps, but this funding was ending, and Seed was in the process of determining how it could best incorporate what it had learned and grow its impact in the future. As Kerry says, "Wyss came in at that time, trusted us, believed in us, understood the vision, understood the mission, and really came in at a meaningful level, which was transformative funding for us. It allowed us to accelerate into the kind of impact that we've now had."[276]

That impact has indeed been enormous. As of 2023, Seed has worked with the government of Uganda to help produce the first physicians in the country who are trained in emergency medicine. These doctors in turn are training others, building up an indigenous capacity that over time will hopefully render Seed's continuing interventions unnecessary. Other Seed projects have taken root in Malawi, Sierra Leone, and Zambia. All told, during 2022–2023 the organization trained over 3,500 health-care workers at seventeen clinical sites serving a population of over seventy million people.[277] These are workers on the front lines, having a direct impact. In Sierra Leone, Seed helped to improve the training of nurse midwives, contributing to a 60 percent drop in maternal deaths in the two hospitals where Seed partners. Kerry tells the story of one health-care professional trained by the organization who saved the life of a mother who tragically had lost her child due to a ruptured uterus. Because the health-care professional had used what she'd learned, this woman had five other children at home who would see their mother again. Without such skilled training, she likely would have died.[278]

Here again is a program that conforms to many of the parameters that make up Wyss's pragmatic approach to choosing projects: It has a big impact on the problem of health disparities. By training doctors, nurses, and midwives in-country and then putting them in a position to train others, the program's impact promises to be long term. Since Seed partners with African governments to build grassroots capacity, and only operates in countries where the organization has been invited to assist a government that is investing in its health infrastructure at the national level, Seed's work is more feasible within a limited time period than it otherwise would be. Given Seed's existing track record, Wyss could regard it as a trusted partner. And the program has an end game: creating enough well-trained practitioners on the ground in local areas who could, in turn, train others, lifting the entire health system while obviating the need for Seed's services.

As a change-maker, how deliberate are you in deciding where to direct your efforts and resources? Are you clear about what you want to achieve, and have you established firm criteria in your mind about what you will and won't take on? Do you keep an eye out for opportunities that seem poised and ready to deliver the change you seek? Are you willing to say no when a project isn't quite right for you? Will you stand up and hold the collaborating organizations and individuals accountable for results? If the answer to these questions is yes, can you ratchet up your choosiness even more?

Being selective requires intellectual effort, discipline, and seriousness of purpose. But it's vital if you want to change the reality on the ground in lasting, measurable ways. Being choosy prevents you from embracing the wrong opportunities, so you can deploy your resources and energies toward the opportunities that matter most. If you learn how and why to say no, you will become far better equipped when the time comes to say yes.

CONCLUSION

THE YEAR IS 1976. In the town of Urtenen-Schönbühl, not far from the city of Bern, where a boy is at home celebrating his fifth birthday, the doorbell rings. To his delight, it's his uncle, whom he hasn't seen in some time. After hugs and greetings, the uncle announces that he has a surprise: He's going to take the boy somewhere special for his birthday.

They get into the uncle's car, and the uncle drives away from the city center and into the outskirts. It's a beautiful day, with bright sun and clear skies. The boy wonders where they are going. To a favorite toy store? To buy some chocolates? Soon, he hears rumbling sounds and sees objects darting past the car. "I'm taking you to the airport," the uncle says. "Look, there's a plane right there, taking off."

The boy has never been to the airport before, nor has he flown in an airplane. His uncle parks the car and takes him into some buildings and then onto the tarmac. They walk toward a small plane with wings overhanging the cabin—a Cessna.

"This is your surprise," the uncle says. "We're going for a ride."

The boy's uncle opens the plane's door and helps him into the copilot's seat. Then he goes around to the plane's other side, climbs in, and straps them both in. As the boy orients himself, his uncle tells him about the dials, levers, and gauges arrayed before them. As the uncle starts the plane, the engine's roar startles the boy.

"Are you ready?" the uncle asks.

The boy nods.

Decades later, the boy won't remember most of the details from this day, including where precisely the plane flies. He is, after all, very young. He'll remember how proud he feels sitting in the copilot's seat, right beside his uncle, and how eager his uncle is to explain how the plane works. As he will say later, "The feeling in my memory is that feeling we all remember from our childhood when an adult we like, love, or admire gives us full attention. We feel that now we are a team with this person—an exclusive team, ready to conquer the world!"[279]

But what will stay the most strongly with this boy are the views he sees outside the airplane's window as his uncle takes him soaring among the nearby Swiss Alps, which are perennially covered in snow. "I mean, it was just beautiful," the boy will later say. "The mountains, the Swiss Alps, all white. There was still more snow and glaciers than now—the eternal snow, as we called it. And being over them and going around one of the big mountains, probably the Matterhorn or something like that." What will also stay with the boy is the affection his uncle shows him: "He loved kids a lot, and he was very caring. He was very warm to me as a kid."

The Swiss musician Nik Leuthold has a lifetime of memories of his uncle Hansjörg Wyss. He still marvels, for instance, at a remarkably challenging climbing route he once saw Wyss execute during the early 2010s in Spain, at a time when Wyss was both a septuagenarian and a novice climber. There have been family celebrations and many additional rides in Wyss's planes over the years. But few of Leuthold's memories are as precious as that early one of Wyss taking him up in the Cessna, soaring through the Alps, just the two of them. Some uncles neglect to give birthday gifts to their nephews and nieces, or they give gifts that don't carry that much meaning. How generous it was for Wyss to share what was so deeply precious to him: his passion for nature's beauty and flying.

Wyss has spent most of his adult life sharing this passion for big, pristine landscapes not just with his family but with the world. Since making that first visit to the United States in 1958, he has done more than just about anyone not only to keep open spaces in the American West intact and wild but to make them publicly accessible for future generations. Concerned about the planet's health, he has taken his approach to conservation global, pledging $1.5 billion to safeguard tens of millions of pristine acres around the world, again with the intention of placing these lands in the public trust for local populations to enjoy. Wyss has given not merely his wealth to preserve wild spaces but also his time and energy. The impact has been enormous: a hundred million acres saved; a new system of public land preservation in the United States overseen by the Bureau of Land Management and supported by a network of grassroots groups; protection and enhancement of the Land and Water Conservation Fund; a pipeline of young leaders dedicated to fighting for land conservation; and a global community energized around the 30x30 goal.

These accomplishments alone would be impressive enough for a single person to have produced, even one of Wyss's wealth. But Wyss has done so much more to effect positive change, impacting the lives of millions of people around the world. He has helped to revolutionize orthopedic surgery, making it dramatically easier, less disruptive, and less costly to heal from bone fractures. He has created and scaled a whole new model for translating scientific breakthroughs into medical innovations, opening up a pipeline of innovations that promise to save lives. He has looked out for society's underdogs, both in the United States and around the world, making gifts to feed the hungry, provide access to medical care for those lacking it, protect the health and welfare of women, and more. He has supported arts institutions that make some of the world's greatest masterpieces available to a wider audience.

Wyss's record of accomplishment inspires us to demand more of the successful people in our midst. Today, the top 1 percent account for about half of all wealth globally, and just eighty-one billionaires together are richer than half of the world's people combined.[280] Yet despite such staggering inequality, the wealthiest among us don't seem to feel much personal responsibility for solving society's problems. Remember, fewer than 10 percent of billionaires have signed the Giving Pledge. By one calculation, members of the 2023 Forbes 400 list of the wealthiest Americans have given away less than 6 percent of their combined net worth. "The members of The Forbes 400 have made a lot of money," the magazine observes. "They haven't given all that much of it away."[281]

Wyss shows us what the wealthiest among us can achieve if they put their minds to it, and it isn't simply about writing big checks. It's about engaging deeply with the world, identifying important problems that affect people and the planet, and using our talents to craft and execute effective solutions. It's also about getting serious and showing some good, old-fashioned virtue. Wyss has his flaws, but he is deeply humble and civic-minded. He sees himself as an ordinary guy, cares deeply about the welfare of ordinary people, and takes seriously his responsibility to use his wealth for social good. Wyss truly is the most impactful person you've never heard of, and his distaste for the limelight has made him *more* effective, not less. By allowing others to take most of the credit, he can concentrate on what really matters: having an impact. The world today needs many more like him.

It isn't only the wealthy who have something to learn from Wyss. It's all of us. From Wyss's life, we can derive a playbook that we can use to achieve the most change possible given the resources at our disposal. Wyss has accomplished so much not because he is unusually intelligent or a subject-matter expert in esoteric fields, and not because he has been particularly idealistic, but because he has proceeded in a disciplined, practical way that arose out of and reflects his middle-class sensibility. He has looked at the world skeptically and has been willing to entertain "crazy" solutions. He has forged big goals for himself in areas that mean something to him. He has avoided distractions and focused on making efficient use of his resources. He has immersed himself in the details and worked across disciplinary boundaries. He has avoided pretension and connected with others on a human level. He has found ways to compensate for his blind spots. He has focused on empowering ordinary people to fight for what is theirs and on building a younger generation of people to lead them. He has persisted with his change-making efforts, challenging himself over time to take on ever bigger and broader goals.

All of us can adopt these behaviors and ways of thinking to make more of a positive difference in the world. Think back to each chapter in this book. How might the lesson apply to the work you're already doing as a change-maker? Are there new steps you can take to make your efforts more effective? If the lesson feels familiar to you, might you rededicate yourself to behaviors that are already working, finding ways to intensify or broaden them?

Wyss's real gift to his five-year-old nephew wasn't an exhilarating ride in a small plane. It was the chance to experience the kind of mind expansion that comes with soaring through the clouds. Throughout his life, Wyss escaped the close confines of his everyday life by exposing himself to massive landscapes, whether it was on a hiking trail through a national monument or soaring at thirty thousand feet. Confronted with the majesty of nature, he found that vast new possibilities opened for him. A sense of the importance of such an expansive vision might well be his ultimate gift to us.

Wyss reminds us of all that becomes possible when we venture beyond the familiar, challenging ourselves to cast aside our traditional beliefs as well as our hubris and to take in the true vastness of creation. Before we can change anything about our circumstances or the challenges that afflict others, we must first accomplish what Wyss has done so effortlessly throughout his life. We must learn to see the world around us with fresh eyes—over and over and over again.

ACKNOWLEDGMENTS

THE AUTHORS WISH TO thank Mr. Hansjörg Wyss for authorizing this project and for enthusiastically supporting it during all of its phases.

We wish to acknowledge a debt of gratitude to the many friends, relatives, colleagues, and associates of Mr. Wyss who agreed to be interviewed for this book. Thank you very much for your time and candor. A big thank you goes to Kris Pauls, Janet Potter, and the team at Disruption Books for their excellent partnership in publishing this book and to Rachel Gostenhofer for help with fact-checking.

Finally, we express our heartfelt gratitude to our families for their ongoing support and encouragement.

NOTES

Introduction

1 "Climbing the Keyhole Route on Longs Peak," Rocky Mountain National Park Media Program Production, video, 4:00, https://www.nps.gov/romo/planyourvisit/longspeak.htm.

2 The company had a second headquarters in Solothurn, Switzerland.

3 In 2011, Synthes had just shy of $4 billion in sales.

4 Catrin Einhorn, "Nearly Every Country Signs On to a Sweeping Deal to Protect Nature," *New York Times*, updated December 20, 2022, https://www.nytimes.com/2022/12/19/climate/biodiversity-cop15-montreal-30x30.html.

5 Thomas Jefferson to Edward Rutledge, December 27, 1796, National Archives, accessed November 14, 2023, https://founders.archives.gov/documents/Jefferson/01-29-02-0189.

Chapter 1

6 This account of Wyss's decision to join Synthes USA is based on interviews with him as well as a Harvard Business School case study on the company: Joseph L. Badaracco Jr. and Richard G. Hamermesh, "Orthoteks USA (A)," HBS 9-384-057 (Boston: Harvard Business School Publishing, 1991).

7 This group has sometimes been known as AO, sometimes as AO/ASIF. We will use both in this book. Please see Jean-Pierre Jeannet, *Leading a Surgical Revolution: The AO Foundation—Social Entrepreneurs in the Treatment of Bone Trauma* (Cham, Switzerland: Springer, 2019), 15.

8 "AO Archive and History," AO Foundation, accessed November 11, 2023, https://www.aofoundation.org/who-we-are/about-ao/ao-archive-and-history.

9 Jean-Pierre Jeannet, *Leading a Surgical Revolution: The AO Foundation—Social Entrepreneurs in the Treatment of Bone Trauma* (Cham, Switzerland: Springer, 2019), 117.

10 Jeannet, *Leading a Surgical Revolution*, 158.

11 Jeannet, *Leading a Surgical Revolution*, 254.

12 The two did meet for breakfast ten years afterward, in 1987, and Wyss was vindicated. As he was happy to inform Zehnder, his seemingly doomed little start-up had grown exponentially under his watch and was now bringing in $64 million in revenues each year. More important, Synthes was making a significant social impact, dramatically improving fracture care in the United States. Thanks to the company's efforts, the standard of care for fractures had flipped, now favoring internal fixation over old-fashioned immobilization. Jeannet, *Leading a Surgical Revolution*, 254–55.

13 Sarah Berger, "Here's What CEOs Actually Do All Day," CNBC, June 20, 2018, https://www.cnbc.com/2018/06/20/harvard-study-what-ceos-do-all-day.html.

14 Robi Frigg, interview with the authors, July 20, 2023. See also "Locking Plate Principles," AO Surgery Reference, accessed November 11, 2023, https://surgeryreference.aofoundation.org/cmf/basic-technique/locking-plate-principles.

15 Marcey Olajos (longtime friend and former romantic partner of Hansjörg Wyss), interview with the authors, April 19, 2023.

16 Joseph L. Badaracco Jr. and Richard G. Hamermesh, "Orthoteks USA (A)," HBS 9-384-057 (Boston: Harvard Business School Publishing, 1991).

17 Steve Schwartz (former Synthes executive and director of Wyss Medical Foundation), interview with the authors, April 27, 2023.

Chapter 2

18 Rick Gennett (former national sales manager at Synthes), interview with the authors, August 4, 2023.

19 Gennett, interview.

20 Jean-Pierre Jeannet, *Leading a Surgical Revolution: The AO Foundation—Social Entrepreneurs in the Treatment of Bone Trauma* (Cham, Switzerland: Springer, 2019), 254, 257.

21 "Rick Gennett," The Org, accessed November 11, 2023, https://theorg.com/org/revbio/org-chart/rick-gennett.

22 See Ranjay Gulati, *Deep Purpose: The Heart and Soul of High-Performance Companies* (New York: Harper Business, 2022).

23 Kyle O'Brien, "Brands Are Facing the 'Age of Cynicism,' from Skeptical Consumers," *Adweek*, May 25, 2021, https://www.adweek.com/agencies/brands-are-facing-the-age-of-cynicism-from-skeptical-consumers/.

24 Christoph Megert (Hansjörg Wyss's attorney and longtime confidant), interview with the authors, May 17, 2023.

25 Debbie Davis (Hansjörg Wyss's longtime assistant), interview with the authors, June 15, 2023.

26 Alexandra Tremayne-Pengelly, "The Young Billionaires Who've Pledged Away Their Wealth," *The Observer*, June 9, 2023, https://observer.com/2023/06/young-billionaires-of-the-giving-pledge/; Oliver Povey, "How Many Billionaires Are There in the World in 2023?" *AS*, updated May 10, 2023, https://en.as.com/latest_news/how-many-billionaires-are-there-in-the-world-in-2023-n/.

27 Josh Bivens and Jori Kandra, "CEO Pay Has Skyrocketed 1,460% Since 1978," Economic Policy Institute, October 4, 2022, https://www.epi.org/publication/ceo-pay-in-2021/.

28 Megert, interview.

29 Davis, interview.

30 "Thoracic Insufficiency Syndrome," Boston Children's Hospital, accessed November 11, 2023, https://www.childrenshospital.org/conditions/thoracic-insufficiency-syndrome.

31 "Vertical Expandable Prosthetic Titanium Rib (VEPTR)," Children's Hospital of Philadelphia, accessed November 11, 2023, https://www.chop.edu/treatments/vertical-expandable-prosthetic-titanium-rib-veptr; Robert M. Campbell Jr., "VEPTR: Past Experience and the Future of VEPTR Principles," *European Spine Journal* 22, no. 2 (Jan 26, 2013), doi: 10.1007/s00586-013-2671-2.

32 Children's Hospital of Philadelphia, "Children's Hospital of Philadelphia Establishes Wyss/Campbell Center for Thoracic Insufficiency Syndrome," PR Newswire, press release, October 17, 2019, https://www.prnewswire.com/news-releases/childrens-hospital-of-philadelphia-establishes-wysscampbell-center-for-thoracic-insufficiency-syndrome-300940826.html.

33 "About the Center for Thoracic Insufficiency Syndrome," Children's Hospital of Philadelphia, accessed November 11, 2023, https://www.chop.edu/centers-programs/center-thoracic-insufficiency-syndrome/about.

34 Andre Mueller (former Synthes board member), interview with the authors, September 5, 2023.

35 Steve Schwartz (former Synthes executive and director of Wyss Medical Foundation), interview with the authors, April 27, 2023.

36 Amin Khoury (former Synthes board member), interview with the authors, August 21, 2023.

37 Eric Lohrer (former Synthes employee), interview with the authors, May 4, 2023.

38 Lohrer, interview.

39 Khoury, interview.

40 Dr. Robert Teitge (surgeon), interview with the authors, August 30, 2023.

41 Teitge, interview.

42 Schwartz, interview.

43 Dr. Robert Teitge, email correspondence with the authors, September 3, 2023.

44 Schwartz, interview.

45 Lohrer, interview.

46 Lohrer, interview.

47 Lohrer, interview.

48 Gennett, interview.

Chapter 3

49 Rick Gennett (former national sales manager at Synthes), interview with the authors, August 4, 2023.

50 Synthes, Inc., filed to SEC Pursuant to Rule 424(b)(3), Registration No. 333-175396 (October 27, 2011), https://www.sec.gov/Archives/edgar/data/200406/000095012311093402/y91766b3e424b3.htm#Y91766126.

51 Caroline Banton, "Just in Case (JIC): What It Is, How It Works, Examples," Investopedia, updated October 28, 2021, https://www.investopedia.com/terms/j/jic.asp.

52 Caroline Banton, "Just-in-Time (JIT): Definition, Example, and Pros & Cons," Investopedia, updated March 14, 2023, https://www.investopedia.com/terms/j/jit.asp.

53 "Hedblom (A)," business case study prepared by L'Institut pour l'Etude des Methodes de Direction de l'Entreprise (IMEDE), Lausanne, Switzerland, 1968. This portion of text also draws on subsequent updates to this case study.

54 "Hedblom (A)," IMEDE business case study.

55 "Hedblom (A)," IMEDE business case study.

56 Gennett, interview.

57 Marcey Olajos (Hansjörg Wyss's longtime friend and former romantic partner), interview with the authors, April 19, 2023.

58 Gennett, interview.

59 Gennett, interview.

60 Molly McUsic (Wyss Foundation president), interview with the authors, April 3, 2023.

Chapter 4

61 Eric Lohrer (former Synthes employee), interview with the authors, May 4, 2023.

62 Lohrer, interview.

63 Lohrer, interview.

64 Rick Gennett (former national sales manager at Synthes), interview with the authors, August 4, 2023.

65 Debbie Davis (Hansjörg Wyss's longtime assistant), interview with the authors, June 15, 2023.

66 Steve Schwartz (former Synthes executive and director of Wyss Medical Foundation), interview with the authors, April 19, 2023.

67 Steve Schwartz (former Synthes executive and director of Wyss Medical Foundation), interview with the authors, April 27, 2023.

68 Rosamund Stone Zander (Hansjörg Wyss's wife and best-selling author), interview with the authors, July 13, 2023.

69 Marcey Olajos (Hansjörg Wyss's longtime friend and former romantic partner), interview with the authors, April 19, 2023.

70 Davis, interview.

71 Olajos, interview.

Chapter 5

72 Jean-Pierre Jeannet, *Leading a Surgical Revolution: The AO Foudnation—Social Entrepreneurs in the Treatment of Bone Trauma* (Cham, Switzerland: Springer, 2019), 257.

73 Christoph Megert (Hansjörg Wyss's attorney and longtime confidant), interview with the authors, May 17, 2023.

74 Shira Ovide, "The Myth of the Genius Tech Inventor," *New York Times*, updated May 8, 2022, https://www.nytimes.com/2022/05/04/technology/myth-of-the-genius-tech-inventor.html; Christopher Mims, "The Myth of the Tech God Is Crumbling," *The Wall Street Journal*, November 19, 2022, https://www.wsj.com/articles/tech-gods-silicon-valley-elon-musk-twitter-sam-bankman-fried-ftx-sbf-11668803154.

75 Bob Bland (former Synthes board member), interview with the authors, May 18, 2023.

76 Felix Pardo (former Synthes board member), interview with the authors, August 10, 2023.

77 Andre Mueller (former Synthes board member), interview with the authors, September 5, 2023.

78 Bland, interview.

79 Mueller, interview.

80 Megert, interview.

81 Mueller, interview.

82 Steve Schwartz (former Synthes executive and director of Wyss Medical Foundation), interview with the authors, July 19, 2023.

83 Robin Young, "How JNJ Bought Synthes and How It Almost Didn't Happen," RRY, July 24, 2012, https://ryortho.com/2012/07/how-jnj-bought-synthes-and-how-it-almost-didnrsquot-happen-part-i/; Anupreeta Das, Gina Chon, and Jonathan D. Rockoff, "J&J to Buy Synthes for $21.3 Billion," *The Wall Street Journal*, April 27, 2011, https://www.wsj.com/articles/SB10001424052748704729304576287622474502438.

84 Johnson & Johnson, "Johnson & Johnson and Synthes Announce Definitive Merger Agreement to Create World's Most Innovative and Comprehensive Orthopaedics Business," press release, April 27, 2011, https://www.jnj.com/media-center/press-releases/johnson-johnson-and-synthes-announce-definitive-merger-agreement-to-create-worlds-most-innovative-and-comprehensive-orthopaedics-business; Johnson & Johnson, "Johnson & Johnson Announces Completion of Synthes Acquisition, Combination Creates the World's Leading Orthopaedics Business," PR Newswire, press release, June 14, 2012, https://www.prnewswire.com/news-releases/johnson--johnson-announces-completion-of-synthes-acquisition-159028985.html.

Chapter 6

85 "Grand Canyon," National Park Service, US Department of the Interior, accessed November 11, 2023, https://www.nps.gov/grca/planyourvisit/upload/royal_arch_loop.pdf.

86 Michael Lanza, "Not Quite Impassable: Backpacking the Grand Canyon's Royal Arch Loop," *The Big Outside*, May 14, 2020, https://thebigoutside.com/not-quite-impassable-back packing-the-grand-canyons-royal-arch-loop/.

87 Jamie Williams (president of The Wilderness Society), interview with the authors, May 25, 2023.

88 Phil Taylor, "'Quietly Philanthropic' Tycoon Makes His Mark in the West," *Greenwire*, March 24, 2015, https://www.eenews.net/articles/quietly-philanthropic-tycoon-makes-his -mark-in-the-west/.

89 Marcey Olajos (Wyss's longtime friend and former romantic partner), interview with the authors, April 19, 2023.

90 "Meet Hansjörg Wyss, National Geographic Philanthropist of the Year," *National Geographic* (blog), July 18, 2019, https://blog.nationalgeographic.org/2019/07/18/meet-hansjorg-wyss -national-geographic-philanthropist-of-the-year/.

91 John Leshy (former US Interior Department general counsel), interview with the authors, April 13, 2023.

92 Theodore Roosevelt, *Outdoor Pastimes of an American Hunter* (University of California Libraries, 1905).

93 Ed Norton (founding president and board member of the Grand Canyon Trust), interview with the authors, June 8, 2023.

94 Rhett A. Butler, "Public Lands and Parks Are Our Common Heritage: Bruce Babbitt," Mongabay, October 22, 2020, https://news.mongabay.com/2020/10/public-lands-and -parks-are-our-common-heritage-an-interview-with-bruce-babbitt/.

95 "American Antiquities Act of 1906: Overview," National Park Service, accessed April 1, 2024, https://www.nps.gov/articles/american-antiquities-act-of-1906.htm; "National Monuments and the Antiquities Act," Congressional Research Service, updated January 2, 2024, https://sgp.fas.org/crs/misc/R41330.pdf.

96 Paul Larmer, ed., *Give and Take: How the Clinton Administration's Public Lands Offensive Transformed the American West* (Colorado: High Country News Books, 2004), 26. The account here of Babbitt, the BLM, and the Conservation Lands Foundation is informed by Heath Alan Nero, "Protected Landscapes and Multiple Use: BLM's National Monuments and Conservation System" (MS thesis, University of Michigan, April 2009), chapter III; Ed Marston, "Interior View: Bruce Babbitt Took the Real West to Washington: A High Country News Interview," *High Country News*, February 12, 2001, https://www.hcn.org/issues/issue -196/interior-view/.

97 Nero, "Protected Landscapes and Multiple Use," 61.

98 Larmer, *Give and Take*, 7.

99 Internal document, Wyss Foundation.

100 Geoff Webb (former CEO of the Wyss Foundation), interview with the authors, July 26, 2023.

101 Molly McUsic, remarks to The Wilderness Society after it awarded its Robert Marshall Prize to Hansjörg Wyss, Museum of the American Indian, Washington, DC, June 8, 2011.

102 Mark Squillace, "The Monumental Legacy of the Antiquities Act of 1906," *Georgia Law Review* 37 (2003): 473–607.

103 Larmer, *Give and Take,* 123.

104 Chris Killingsworth (Wyss Foundation executive vice president) and Heath Nero (senior program officer at the Wyss Foundation and former Wyss Scholar), interview with the authors, April 20, 2023; "Cheney Says Some National Monument Decisions Could Be Rescinded," *The Record-Courier*, December 19, 2001, https://www.recordcourier.com/news/2001/dec/19/cheney-says-some-national-monument-decisions-could/.

105 "Bush Will Not Overturn Monuments," ABC News, February 21, 2001, https://abcnews.go.com/Politics/story?id=121803&page=1.

106 Killingsworth and Nero, interview.

107 Norton, interview.

108 Killingsworth and Nero, interview.

109 Clifford Rechtschaffen, "The Bush Record on the Environment: What a Difference Two Years Make," Golden Gate University School of Law, Class Action (Spring 2003): 2–10. See also Emily Cousins, Robert Perks, and Wesley Warren, "Rewriting the Rules Special Edition: The Bush Administration's First-Term Environmental Record," Natural Resources Defense Council (January 2005), https://www.nrdc.org/sites/default/files/rr2005.pdf.

110 John D. Leshy, "Still Made for You and Me? Our Public Lands Are Under Attack as Never Before by the Trump Administration," *The American Scholar*, September 14, 2020, https://theamericanscholar.org/still-made-for-you-and-me/.

111 James William Gibson, "Cleaning Up Bush's Mess on Public Land," *Los Angeles Times*, April 2, 2009, https://www.latimes.com/opinion/la-oe-gibson2-2009apr02-story.html.

112 Speech of Hon. Abraham Lincoln at Ottawa, Northern Illinois University Digital Library, August 31, 1858, https://digital.lib.niu.edu/islandora/object/niu-lincoln%3A38360.

113 John Leshy, "America's Public Lands: A Sketch of Their Political History and Future Challenges," *Natural Resources Journal* 62, no. 2 (summer 2022): 356, https://digital repository.unm.edu/cgi/viewcontent.cgi?article=4130&context=nrj.

114 John Leshy (former US Interior Department official), interview with the authors, April 13, 2023.

115 McUsic, remarks to The Wilderness Society.

Chapter 7

116 Chris Montgomery, Rick Graetz, and Susie Graetz, "This Is Montana," University of Montana, accessed November 11, 2023, https://www.umt.edu/this-is-montana/columns/stories/centennialvalley.php.

117 Montgomery, Graetz, and Graetz, "This Is Montana."

118 "The Centennial Valley," The Nature Conservancy, accessed November 11, 2023, https://www.nature.org/en-us/get-involved/how-to-help/places-we-protect/centennial-valley/; Montgomery, Graetz, and Graetz, "This Is Montana."

119 "Range Riding in Montana's Wild Centennial Valley," Greater Yellowstone Coalition, October 14, 2021, https://greateryellowstone.org/blog/2021/centennialvalley; "The Centennial Valley," The Nature Conservancy.

120 "The Centennial Valley," The Nature Conservancy.

121 John Leshy (former US Interior Department official), interview with the authors, August 29, 2023.

122 Jim Baca, "Great Places," *Only in New Mexico* (blog), August 25, 2006, http://onlyinnewmexico.blogspot.com/2006/08/great-places.html.

123 Leshy, interview.

124 Jamie Williams (president of The Wilderness Society), interview with the authors, May 25, 2023.

125 Eric Lohrer (former Synthes employee), interview with the authors, April 26, 2023.

126 Jill Johnson, "Four Ways Land Conservation Mitigates the Impact of Climate Change," Conservation Foundation, July 15, 2020, https://www.theconservationfoundation.org/four-ways-land-conservation-mitigates-the-impact-of-climate-change/.

127 "Crown of the Continent Ecosystem," Trust for Public Land, accessed November 11, 2023, https://www.tpl.org/our-work/crown-continent-ecosystem.

128 "Conservationists Go Big in Montana," The Wyss Foundation, July 3, 2011, https://www.wyssfoundation.org/news/conservationists-go-big-in-montana-land-and-people.

129 "Conservationists Go Big," The Wyss Foundation.

130 Williams, interview.

131 Mackenzie Reiss, "Historic Holland Lake Lodge Up for Sale," *Daily Inter Lake*, October 6, 2019, https://dailyinterlake.com/news/2019/oct/06/historic-holland-lake-lodge-up-for-sale-6/.

132 Williams, interview.

133 "Oil Company Agrees to Relinquish Oil Lease Near Glacier National Park Share," *National Parks Traveler*, October 4, 2019, https://www.nationalparkstraveler.org/2019/10/oil-company-agrees-relinquish-oil-lease-near-glacier-national-park. This account also relies on a conversation with John Leshy (August 29, 2023).

134 David Carr (longtime employee, The Nature Conservancy in Montana), interview with the authors, May 15, 2023.

135 "Support Helps Conserve Montana's Blackfoot River Valley," Wyss Foundation, January 22, 2015, https://www.wyssfoundation.org/news/wyss-foundations-support-helps-conserve-117000-acres-in-montanas-blackfoot-river-valley.

136 Chris Killingsworth (executive vice president, Wyss Foundation), interview with the authors, July 21, 2023.

137 Carr, interview.

138 Williams, interview.

139 "Land and Water Conservation Fund," US Department of the Interior, accessed November 14, 2023, https://www.doi.gov/lwcf.

140 "Land and Water Conservation Fund: Overview, Funding History, and Issues," Congressional Research Office, updated August 17, 2018, https://crsreports.congress.gov/product/pdf/RL/RL33531/25.

141 "Time for Full Funding for LWCF," Land and Water Conservation Fund, April 16, 2019, https://lwcfcoalition.org/blog/2019/4/10/time-for-full-funding-for-lwcf.

142 Andy French (conservation program officer, Wyss Foundation), interview with the authors, September 13, 2023.

143 French, interview.

144 Kerry Leslie, "After 55 Years, Land and Water Conservation Fund Is Now Permanently, Fully Funded," The Wilderness Society, August 4, 2020, https://www.wilderness.org/news/press-release/after-55-years-land-and-water-conservation-fund-now-permanently-fully-funded.

Chapter 8

145 "John Day Wild and Scenic River," Bureau of Land Management, accessed November 11, 2023, https://www.blm.gov/programs/recreation/permits-and-passes/lotteries-and-permit-systems/oregon-washington/john-day-river.

146 "McDonald's Ferry John Day River," Western Rivers Conservancy, accessed November 11, 2023, https://www.westernrivers.org/projects/or/john-day-river-mcdonalds-ferry.

147 "About," Western Rivers Conservancy, accessed November 11, 2023, https://www.westernrivers.org/about.

148 Alex Barton (conservationist), interview with the authors, August 30, 2023.

149 *McDonald's Ferry Ranch on the Wild and Scenic John Day River*, informational pamphlet, Western Rivers Conservancy, n.d.

150 Barton, interview.

151 "The Wyss Scholars Program," Wyss Foundation, accessed November 11, 2023, https://www.wyssfoundation.org/scholars. Those studying for a law degree receive a third of their costs and tuition.

152 Heath Nero (senior program officer at the Wyss Foundation and former Wyss Scholar), interview with the authors, August 8, 2023.

153 Kellie Shanaghan (conservation program associate, Wyss Foundation), interview with the authors, August 8, 2023.

154 "Julia Elkin (MS '15)," School of Environment and Sustainability University of Michigan, accessed November 11, 2023, https://seas.umich.edu/alumni/alumni-stories/julia-elkin-ms-15.

155 Grecia Nunez (former Wyss Fellow), interview with the authors, August 28, 2023.

156 Brent Fenty (executive director, Oregon Desert Land Trust), interview with the authors, August 29, 2023.

157 "Wyss Scholars Program Supports Future Western Conservation Leaders," Yale School of the Environment, accessed November 11, 2023, https://environment.yale.edu/news/article/wyss-foundation-scholarships-support-future-western-leaders.

158 Nero, interview.

159 Greg Zimmerman (director of the Protection Campaign at the Resources Legacy Fund and former Wyss Scholar at Yale), interview with the authors, September 6, 2023.

Chapter 9

160 Brown University, "Extinctions during Human Era Worse Than Thought," *News from Brown* (blog), September 2, 2014, https://news.brown.edu/articles/2014/09/extinctions.

161 Elizabeth Kolbert, *The Sixth Extinction: An Unnatural History* (New York: Henry Holt and Co., 2014).

162 Chris Killingsworth (executive vice president, Wyss Foundation), interview with the authors, July 21, 2023.

163 Brian O'Donnell (former executive director of the Conservation Lands Foundation and executive director of the Campaign for Nature), interview with the authors, April 26, 2023.

164 Edward O. Wilson, *Half-Earth: Our Planet's Fight for Life* (New York: Liveright, 2016).

165 Stephen Woodley, Harvey Locke, Dan Laffoley, Kathy MacKinnon, Trevor Sandwith, and Jane Smart, "A Review of Evidence for Area-Based Conservation Targets for the Post-2020 Global Biodiversity Framework," *Parks* 25, no. 2 (November 2019): 31–46, https://www.researchgate.net/publication/338522157_A_review_of_evidence_for_area-based_conservation_targets_for_the_post-2020_global_biodiversity_framework.

166 O'Donnell, interview.

167 Molly McUsic (Wyss Foundation president), interview with the authors, April 3, 2023.

168 Wyss Campaign for Nature, "Wyss Foundation Launches $1 Billion Campaign to Help Conserve 30% of the Planet by 2030," PR Newswire, press release, October 31, 2018, https://www.prnewswire.com/news-releases/wyss-foundation-launches-1-billion-campaign-to-help-conserve-30-of-the-planet-by-2030-300741327.html.

169 Hansjörg Wyss, "We Have to Save the Planet. So I'm Donating $1 Billion," *New York Times*, October 31, 2018, https://www.nytimes.com/2018/10/31/opinion/earth-biodiversity-conservation-billion-dollars.html.

170 Heath Nero (senior program officer at the Wyss Foundation and former Wyss Scholar), interview with the authors, March 28, 2023.

171 O'Donnell, interview.

172 O'Donnell, interview.

173 Catrin Einhorn, "Nearly Every Country Signs On to a Sweeping Deal to Protect Nature," *New York Times*, updated December 20, 2022, https://www.nytimes.com/2022/12/19/climate/biodiversity-cop15-montreal-30x30.html; Lindsay Maizland, "The Push to Conserve 30 Percent of the Planet: What's at Stake?" Council on Foreign Relations, updated March 6, 2023, https://www.cfr.org/article/goal-conserve-30-percent-planet-2030-biodiversity-climate.

174 League of Conservation Voters, "450 State and Local Elected Officials Declare Support for Protecting 30% of America's Land and Ocean by 2030," press release, January 26, 2021, https://www.lcv.org/media-center/450-state-and-local-elected-officials-declare-support-for-protecting-30-of-americas-land-and-ocean-by-2030/.

175 "$20 Billion Tracker," Nature Finance Info, October 2, 2023, https://www.naturefinance.info/.

176 "Support for 30x30," Campaign for Nature, accessed April 1, 2024, https://www.campaignfornature.org/support-for-30x30-1.

177 "G20 Leaders Must Give Prominence to Finance for Nature in the Leaders Declaration and Chart a Path to Delivering on the Kunming-Montreal Global Biodiversity Framework," Campaign for Nature, August 31, 2023, https://www.campaignfornature.org/joint-ngo-statement-on-g20-leaders-summit; "Former Heads of Government Call on African Climate Summit: Ensure $20 Billion Nature Finance Promise by 2025 Is Prioritized," Campaign for Nature, accessed November 12, 2023, https://www.campaignfornature.org/gsc-urge-leaders-at-africa-climate-summit-to-prioritize-nature.

178 Maizland, "The Push to Conserve 30 Percent of the Planet."

179 O'Donnell, interview.

Chapter 10

180 The authors draw heavily here on Jonathan Shaw, "Hansjörg Wyss Boosts Bioengineering Innovation," *Harvard Magazine*, June 7, 2019, https://www.harvardmagazine.com/2019/06/wyss-gift-of-131-million.

181 Shaw, "Hansjörg Wyss Boosts Bioengineering Innovation."

182 Steve Hyman (former Harvard provost), interview with the authors, May 23, 2023.

183 Hyman, interview.

184 Hyman, interview.

185 Don Ingber (Wyss Institute, founding director), interview with the authors, April 18, 2023.

186 Ingber, interview.

187 Mary Tolikas, Ayis Antoniou, and Don Ingber, "The Wyss Institute: A New Model for Medical Technology Innovation and Translation across the Academic-Industrial Interface," *Bioengineering and Translational Medicine* 5, no. 3 (September 2017): 247–57, https://pub med.ncbi.nlm.nih.gov/29313034/.

188 Hyman, interview.

189 "$125-Million Gift for Bioengineering," *Harvard Magazine*, October 7, 2008, https://www .harvardmagazine.com/2008/10/125-million-gift-for-bioengineering

190 Tolikas, Antoniou, and Ingber, "The Wyss Institute," 3–4.

191 Shaw, "Hansjörg Wyss Boosts Bioengineering Innovation."

192 Tolikas, Antoniou, and Ingber, "The Wyss Institute," 4.

193 "James J. Collins Elected a Member of the National Academy of Engineering," Wyss Institute, February 9, 2011, https://wyss.harvard.edu/news/james-j-collins-elected-a-member -of-the-national-academy-of-engineering/; Don Ingber, email correspondence with the authors, September 30, 2023.

194 Tolikas, Antoniou, and Ingber, "The Wyss Institute," 9.

195 Courtney Humphries, "Designing from Life," *Harvard Magazine*, May–June 2011, https ://www.harvardmagazine.com/2011/04/designing-from-life.

196 Daniel Levner (engineer at the Weiss Institute), interview with the authors, April 21, 2023.

197 "Facts and Statistics about Animal Testing," PETA, accessed November 12, 2023, https ://www.peta.org/issues/animals-used-for-experimentation/animals-used-experimentation -factsheets/animal-experiments-overview/.

198 Tolikas, Antoniou, and Ingber, "The Wyss Institute," 5–6.

199 Levner, interview.

200 Levner, interview.

201 "14 Years of Technology Innovation," Wyss Institute.

202 "14 Years of Technology Innovation," Wyss Institute.

203 Ingber, interview.

204 "Celebrating Visionary Philanthropy," Wyss Institute, video, 1:43:23, https://vimeo.com /823535717/c8c897922d.

205 Hyman, interview.

Chapter 11

206 "Health Benefits of Brazil Nuts," Web MD, accessed November 12, 2023, https://www.web md.com/diet/health-benefits-brazil-nuts.

207 "The Most Popular Nuts in the World," World Atlas, accessed November 12, 2023, https: //www.worldatlas.com/articles/the-most-popular-nuts-in-the-world.html.

208 "Health Benefits of Brazil Nuts," Web MD, accessed November 12, 2023, https://www.web md.com/diet/health-benefits-brazil-nuts.

209 Elisângela Colpo et al., "A Single Consumption of High Amounts of the Brazil Nuts Improves Lipid Profile of Healthy Volunteers," *Journal of Nutrition and Metabolism* (June 11, 2013), https://www.ncbi.nlm.nih.gov/pmc/articles/PMC3693158/; Justyna Godos et al., "Effect of Brazil Nuts on Selenium Status, Blood Lipids, and Biomarkers of Oxidative Stress and Inflammation: A Systematic Review and Meta-Analysis of Randomized Clinical Trials," *Antioxidants* 11, no. 2 (February 16, 2022), https://www.ncbi.nlm.nih.gov/pmc/articles /PMC8869304/.

210 "Madre de Dios, Peru," World Wildlife Fund, https://www.worldwildlife.org/pages/madre -de-dios-peru.

211 "The Brazil Nut Project (2020)," Wyss Academy for Nature, March 17, 2022, https://www .wyssacademy.org/post/the-brazil-nut-project-2020; Peter Messerli (director of the Wyss Academy for Nature), interview with the authors, September 7, 2023.

212 "What's a Wicked Problem?" Stony Brook University, accessed November 11, 2023, https ://www.stonybrook.edu/commcms/wicked-problem/about/What-is-a-wicked-problem.

213 Messerli, interview.

214 Miguel Saravia, "Improving Human Wellbeing While Preventing Deforestation in the Amazon Rainforest," *Annual Report 2022*, Wyss Academy for Nature, https://annualreport .wyssacademy.org/south-america/interview/improving-human-wellbeing-while-preventing -deforestation-amazon-rainforest.

215 "A Visionary Approach," Wyss Academy for Nature, accessed November 12, 2023, https ://www.wyssacademy.org/vision-and-mision.

216 "Theory of Change," Wyss Academy for Nature, accessed November 12, 2023, https://www .wyssacademy.org/home.

217 The Brain Forum, "Philanthropists for Brain Science," YouTube video, 28:57, March 30, 2015, https://www.youtube.com/watch?v=l8upkDIwTaY.

218 "Billionaire Envisions Swiss Centre as Change Agent," Swiss Info, May 23, 2015, https ://www.swissinfo.ch/eng/business/biotech-boost_billionaire-envisions-swiss-centre-as-change -agent/41447816.

219 The Brain Forum, "Philanthropists for Brain Science."

220 Campus Biotech, informational brochure, June 2019, https://www.campusbiotech.ch/sites /default/files/2019-06/CAMPUS_BIOTECH.pdf.

221 Campus Biotech, informational brochure.

222 "Ability," Wyss Center, accessed November 12, 2023, https://wysscenter.ch/advances/ability.

223 "Soft Neural Implants," Wyss Center, accessed November 2, 2023, https://wysscenter.ch /advances/soft-neural-implants; "Early Detection of Dementia with Smart Imaging," Wyss Center, accessed November 12, 2023, https://wysscenter.ch/advances/early-detection-of -dementia-with-smart-imaging; "Improving Brain Tumor Treatment," Wyss Center, accessed November 12, 2023, https://wysscenter.ch/advances/improving-brain-tumor-treatment; "Repairing the Spinal Cord," Wyss Center, accessed November 12, 2023, https://wysscenter .ch/advances/repairing-the-spinal-cord.

224 "Billionaire's Cash Brings Medical Research to Patients," Swiss Info, accessed November 11, 2023, https://www.swissinfo.ch/eng/wyss-center_billionaire-s-cash-brings-medical-research-to-patients/41824274.

225 "Swiss Universities Launch New Wyss Center," Wyss Foundation, December 15, 2015, https://www.wyssfoundation.org/news/swiss-universities-launch-new-wyss-translational-center-to-advance-science-medicine-and-engineering; Swiss Info, "Billionaire's Cash."

226 ETH Zurich, "ETH and University of Zurich Launch Wyss Translational Center Zurich," press release, December 2014, https://ethz.ch/en/news-and-events/eth-news/news/2014/12/eth-and-university-of-zurich-launch-wyss-translational-center-zurich.html.

227 "World Premiere: Human Liver Treated in Machine Successfully Transplanted," Wyss Zurich, May 31, 2022, https://www.wysszurich.ch/news/world-premiere-human-liver-treated-in-machine-successfully-transplanted.

228 "Tethys Robotics Wins Venture Kick Stage III," Wyss Zurich, September 26, 2023, https://www.wysszurich.ch/news/tethys-wins-venture-kick-stage-iii; "Hylomorph Secures CHF 4.5 Million in Series B2 Financing Round," Wyss Zurich, May 9, 2023, https://www.wysszurich.ch/news/hylomorph-secures-chf-4-5m-in-series-b2-financing-round; "Hemotune Achieves ISO 13485 Certification," Wyss Zurich, August 21, 2023, https://www.wysszurich.ch/news/hemotune-achieves-iso-13485-certification; "Seervision Acquired by California-Based Company Q-SYS," Wyss Zurich, June 12, 2023, https://www.wysszurich.ch/news/seervision-acquired-by-q-sys-a-division-of-qsc-llc; *Wyss Zurich Pocket Guide*, 2023.

229 Gert-Jan Nabuurs et al., "Agriculture, Forestry and Other Land Uses (AFOLU)," in *IPCC: Climate Change 2022: Mitigation of Climate Change*, Contribution of Working Group III to the Sixth Assessment Report of the Intergovernmental Panel on Climate Change, edited by P. R. Shukla et al. (Cambridge University Press, 2022), https://www.ipcc.ch/report/ar6/wg3/chapter/chapter-7/.

230 Messerli, interview.

231 Birgit Voigt, "NZZ Interview with Hansjörg Wyss," Wyss Foundation, April 26, 2019, https://www.wyssfoundation.org/news/in-business-people-tend-to-take-a-short-term-often-very-selfish-view-says-billionaire-hansjrg-wyss.

232 "Wyss Academy for Nature Founded at the University of Bern," Wyss Campaign for Nature, December 13, 2019, https://www.wysscampaign.org/news/2019/12/13/wyss-academy-for-nature-founded-at-the-university-of-bern.

233 Messerli, interview.

234 "Benson Okita Joins the Hub East Africa Team as Hub Director," Wyss Academy for Nature, April 12, 2022, https://www.wyssacademy.org/post/benson-okita.

235 *Annual Report 2022*, Wyss Academy for Nature, accessed November 12, 2023, https://annualreport.wyssacademy.org/#keyfigures.

236 "Local Resource Stewardship in Tropical Forest Frontiers," *Annual Report 2022*, Wyss Academy for Nature, accessed November 12, 2023, https://annualreport.wyssacademy.org/south-east-asia/local-resource-stewardship-tropical-forest-frontiers.

237 "Accelerating the Energy Transition," *Annual Report 2022*, Wyss Academy for Nature, https://annualreport.wyssacademy.org/bern/accelerating-energy-transition.

238 Messerli, interview.

239 "Letter to Our Stakeholders," Wyss Academy for Nature, *Annual Report 2023*, accessed November 12, 2023, https://annualreport.wyssacademy.org/letter-our-stakeholders.

240 Messerli, interview.

Chapter 12

241 Grace Kendall (director of development and engagement, Safe Voices), email correspondence with the authors, July 13, 2023. According to the organization's annual report: "The mission of Safe Voices is to provide person-to-person, individualized advocacy for all survivors of domestic abuse and violence, sex trafficking, and sexual exploitation in Androscoggin, Franklin, and Oxford Counties and engage our communities in social change to eliminate violence."

242 Elise Johansen (executive director, Safe Voices), interview with the authors, July 13, 2023.

243 Kendall, interview.

244 "Who We Are and What We Do," PeaceWomen Across the Globe, accessed November 12, 2023, https://1000peacewomen.org/en/about-us; "More Than a Shelter . . . a Second Chance," Rosie's Place, accessed March 27, 2024, https://www.rosiesplace.org/.

245 "Maternal and Child Health," Seed Global Health, accessed November 12, 2023, https://seedglobalhealth.org/what-we-do/maternal-and-child-health/.

246 Cameron Scott, "Nurse Training Program GAIN Expands with Major Gift," UCSF Institute for Global Health Sciences, July 20, 2020, https://globalhealthsciences.ucsf.edu/blog/nurse-training-program-gain-expands-with-major-gift.

247 A complete listing of donations and donors is available in the HJW Foundation's tax filings (Internal Revenue Form 990) for 2011. The HJW Foundation was dissolved in 2013.

248 Molly McUsic (Wyss Foundation president), interview with the authors, July 17, 2023.

249 "Wyss Wellness Center," accessed November 12, 2023, https://wysswellnesscenter.org/.

250 NYU Langone, "NYU Langone Creates Charity Care Fund for Patients in Need of Complex Reconstructive Plastic Surgery," press release, May 1, 2019, https://nyulangone.org/news/nyu-langone-creates-charity-care-fund-patients-need-complex-reconstructive-plastic-surgery; Marla Lehner, "A Partnership Based on Common Goals," Children's Hospital Los Angeles, December 9, 2020, https://www.chla.org/blog/partnership-based-common-goals.

251 "About the Center," Center on Budget and Policy Priorities, accessed November 12, 2023, https://www.cbpp.org/about.

252 "Preserving the Rights and Freedoms of All in America and Protecting Our Judiciary," Constitutional Accountability Center, accessed November 12, 2023, https://www.theusconstitution.org/about-cac/; "Fighting for Health Rights for All," National Health Law Program, accessed November 12, 2023, https://healthlaw.org/; "About Us," Washington Center for Equitable Growth, accessed November 12, 2023, https://equitablegrowth.org/who-we-are/about-us/; "Grant in the Spotlight: Georgetown University Center for Children and Families," Wyss Foundation, April 24, 2023, https://www.wyssfoundation.org/news/grant-in-the-spotlight-georgetown-university-center-for-children-and-families; Heather C. McGhee, Lucy Mayo, and Angela Park, "Demos' Racial Equity Transformation: Key Components, Process & Lessons," Demos, November 15, 2018, https://www.demos.org/research/demos-racial-equity-transformation-key-components-process-lessons.

253 *Annual Report 2022*, AO Alliance, July 2023, https://ao-alliance.org/wp-content/uploads/2023/07/aoa_annual-report-2022_final-1.pdf.

254 AO Alliance, https://ao-alliance.org.

255 AO Alliance, https://ao-alliance.org.

256 Children's Hospital of Los Angeles, *Philanthropic Impact Report* for the Wyss Foundation, 2023; Alex Carter (senior vice president and chief development officer, Children's Hospital of Los Angeles), interview with the authors, July 19, 2023.

257 Kimberly Baltzell (professor, University of San Francisco School of Nursing and Health Professions), email correspondence with the authors, August 11, 2023.

258 Ulf Küster (senior curator, Fondation Beyeler), interview with the authors, May 17, 2023.

259 "Mission Statement," Fondation Beyeler, accessed November 12, 2023, https://www.fondationbeyeler.ch/en/museum/mission-statement.

260 "Grant in the Spotlight: Fondation Beyeler," Wyss Foundation, November 4, 2021, https://www.wyssfoundation.org/news/grant-in-the-spotlight-fondation-beyeler.

Chapter 13

261 Marc Altshuler (primary care physician), interview with the authors, July 13, 2023.

262 Altshuler, interview.

263 Steve Schwartz (former Synthes executive and director of Wyss Medical Foundation), interview with the authors, June 12, 2023.

264 Laura Bryski, "Now Open at Bok, a New Health Center for Philly's Immigrant and Refugee Population," *Philadelphia*, April 29, 2021, https://www.phillymag.com/healthcare-news/2021/04/29/hansjorg-wyss-wellness-center-bok-building/.

265 Altshuler, interview.

266 Bryski, "Now Open at Bok."

267 "Center for Refugee and Immigrant Health," Thomas Jefferson University, accessed November 12, 2023, https://jefferson.edu/academics/colleges-schools-institutes/skmc/departments/family-medicine/divisions-special-programs/center-for-refugee-health.html.

268 "Jefferson Announces Gift to the Hansjörg Wyss Wellness Center," Jefferson Health, June 7, 2023, https://www.jeffersonhealth.org/about-us/news/2023/06/gift-to-wyss-wellness-center; Hansjörg Wyss Wellness Center, *Impact Report*, May 2023.

269 Jefferson Health, "Jefferson Announces Gift."

270 Fatana Bayat (Wyss Center employee and patient), interview with the authors, October 13, 2023.

271 Altshuler, interview.

272 Heath Nero (senior program officer at the Wyss Foundation and former Wyss Scholar), interview with the authors, April 20, 2023.

273 Dr. Jason B. Anari (Children's Hospital of Philadelphia), interview with the authors, August 21, 2023.

274 Kimberly Baltzell (professor, University of San Francisco School of Nursing and Health Professions), interview with the authors, July 26, 2023.

275 "IGHS Global Action in Nursing Receives Renewed Funding from the Wyss Medical Foundation," Institute for Global Health Sciences, September 19, 2022, https://globalhealthsciences.ucsf.edu/news-ighs-global-action-nursing-receives-renewed-funding-wyss-medical-foundation/.

276 Dr. Vanessa Kerry (founder and CEO, Seed Global Health), interview with the authors, August 8, 2023.

277 *Annual Report 2022*, Seed Global Health, July 2023: 4, https://seedglobalhealth.org/wp-content/uploads/2023/07/Seed_2023_Annual-Report_Final.pdf.

278 Kerry, interview.

Conclusion

279 Nik Leuthold (nephew of Hansjörg Wyss), email correspondence with the authors, December 5, 2023.

280 Khanyi Mlaba, "The Richest 1% Own Almost Half the World's Wealth and 9 Other Mind-Blowing Facts on Wealth Inequality," *Global Citizen*, January 19, 2023, https://www.globalcitizen.org/en/content/wealth-inequality-oxfam-billionaires-elon-musk/.

281 Phoebe Liu, "The Forbes Philanthropy Score 2023: How Charitable Are the Richest Americans?" *Forbes*, October 3, 2023, https://www.forbes.com/sites/phoebeliu/2023/10/03/the-forbes-philanthropy-score-2023-how-charitable-are-the-richest-americans/?sh=1b0f8b46eccc.

ABOUT THE AUTHORS

PAUL ORZULAK

Paul Orzulak is an executive director and cofounder of West Wing Writers, America's premier strategy and speechwriting firm. He served as a foreign policy speechwriter for President Bill Clinton and a domestic policy speechwriter for Vice President Al Gore. A frequent media contributor, he traces his passion for conservation back to an old boss, Congressman David Bonior, who began distributing free pine seedlings after an ice storm destroyed many of Michigan's trees, and eventually gave out more than a million, a powerful reminder that we do not have to be spectators in the causes we care about.

SETH SCHULMAN

Seth Schulman wields the power of the written word to start conversations, change minds, and transform lives. A master storyteller and intellectual collaborator, he has contributed to dozens of books over the past two decades. Mr. Schulman holds a PhD in intellectual and cultural history from Brown University.